© 2013 Training The Street, Inc.
All rights reserved.

Preparing Financial Professionals for Success
www.trainingthestreet.com

111912

Table of Contents

TRAINING THE STREET

Before We Get Started – Introduction

Welcome to Training The Street's (TTS) Fundamentals of Financial Accounting & Analysis authored by Stephen H. Bryan, Ph.D. This self study Handbook discusses common accounting, reporting and financial analysis issues encountered by professionals required to understand and analyze financial information—from investment bankers and financial analysts to corporate managers and executives.

Chances are that the corporate finance and accounting principles you learned in the classroom had a theoretical twist. They probably lacked the practical emphasis that professionals give these concepts as they use them every day. At TTS we have had years of experience in not only teaching the principles of accounting, but also using these foundational tools in a broad spectrum of financial statement analysis, corporate valuation and financial modeling situations. This Handbook is a compact distillation of most of the practical knowledge you will need to begin analyzing financial statements.

While TTS had beginners and those in need of a refresher in mind with this Handbook, TTS is especially excited about this unique approach because it also includes several intermediate and advanced topics often found in higher level texts. These more complex topics are delivered with the author's intuitive and seamless style such that the reader is unaware that they have just tackled a more difficult area.

Our aim is to teach accounting and financial statement analysis as if you were required to understand and analyze real financial statements for the real world shortly after completing the Handbook. In a lucid, practical way, we lay out the applied components of what you would obtain in a university class, without shortchanging you on any of their most important conceptual underpinnings. As you go through this practical material, however, bear in mind that learning is not about formula memorization, computational manipulation, or mechanical success in reaching the right answer. It is about understanding the underlying concepts, and why you are doing what you are doing. This Handbook and the Companion Book, "Real World Analysis & Exercises", each contain a box of razor-sharp tools, and also sets up each tool within the practical contexts in which they are used.

Companion Book "Real World Analysis & Exercises":

1) Real World Analysis Case Study
2) Practice Exercises (and Solutions)

Please check our website at www.trainingthestreet.com for other self-study products and live instruction alternatives such as Corporate Valuation, Financial Modeling, Excel Best Practices and many more to come.

SPECIAL FEATURES – How to Use This Handbook

Hotwords You will come across ◀**hotwords**▶ throughout the Handbook. These words, bolded and bracketed in solid arrowheads, are terms widely used in financial analysis, corporate finance and M&A work. They can be looked up in the Hotword Glossary at the end of the Handbook.

Key Formulas To accelerate learning, we have also identified key formulas we regard as especially critical to performing analysis and understanding relationships essential for financial modeling. You will recognize them by the "key" icon next to them.

Practice Exercises For each chapter of the Handbook please check out the Companion Book "Real World Analysis & Exercises", where we've delivered over 150 practice exercises and knowledge checks to complement the Handbook lessons and solidify your learning experience. Once you've challenged yourself, check and see if you got the correct answers!

Text Boxes Finally, throughout the Handbook there are sidebars, mini-case studies, and text boxes that address commonly asked questions, explain unfamiliar phrases, and offer you useful tips and fill-ins. Throughout the chapters, you will find the following:

Ask the Finance Guru boxes present questions to which we have invited TTS experts to respond and share their thoughts. Because we train thousands of finance professionals every year, we have an experienced viewpoint in addressing the questions that puzzle students and practitioners alike. We have drawn on this reservoir of experience to frame and answer some of the most commonly posed questions.

Tips of the Trade and A Bit of Perspective sidebars provide you with practical suggestions, calculation assistance, shortcut tools, how-to tips, and commonly encountered pitfalls and errors you should watch out for.

A Word on Terminology and Words to Know boxes offer you quick or alternative definitions of difficult terms.

A final word of advice before we jump into the thick of things: try to view this Handbook not as a "textbook" but rather as a practical guide that offers you a framework for the kinds of items that will be interpreted when analyzing a firm. Above all, we hope it will help demystify the whole topic of accounting and financial statement analysis by laying out in a truly clear, down-to-earth way the types of analytics a variety of professionals use every day when they go to work.

Have fun!

About the Author Stephen H. Bryan, Ph. D.

Professor Bryan has a Ph.D. in Accounting from New York University's Stern School of Business, as well as M.B.A. and B.S. degrees from Baruch College (City University of New York) and from the University of North Carolina-Chapel Hill, respectively. He is currently on the faculty at Fordham University Schools of Business in New York. Prior tenured faculty positions include Wake Forest University (Winston Salem, North Carolina), and Baruch College. While at Wake Forest, Dr. Bryan led numerous summer business study trips to Central and Eastern Europe. He has designed accounting and finance curricula for financial institutions, law firms, and multinational corporations. He has also had visiting positions on faculties in Vienna, Austria and Frankfurt, Germany.

Professor Bryan's research interests focus on corporate disclosures and corporate governance, and his research has been published in some of the leading academic and professional journals, including the Journal of Corporate Finance, the Accounting Review, the Journal of Business, Harvard Business Review, Financial Management, The Accountants' Handbook, and the Journal of Accounting, Auditing, and Finance. His teaching has been recognized with several awards, including the Kienzle award (from Wake Forest University), which alumni award to the faculty member who most benefited their careers. He is founder and principal of Accounting Analytics, LLC and The Accounting Oasis, LLC, which design and produce curricular materials on accounting issues currently confronting the analyst community and other user groups. Professor Bryan also delivers live seminars as an instructor for TTS. He can be reached at *Stephen.Bryan@TheAccountingOasis.com*.

This Handbook, "Fundamentals of Financial Accounting & Analysis", and its Companion Book, "Real World Analysis & Exercises", are compilations of topics selected by TTS and Professor Bryan to get readers up to speed quickly. For the expanded and complete versions of the Handbook and the Companion Book, please visit Professor Bryan's website *www.theaccountingoasis.com*.

Chapter 1: Introduction to Financial Accounting: The Language of Business

---

THE PURPOSE OF FINANCIAL ACCOUNTING

Financial Accounting is the language of business. Its purpose is to communicate financial information to interested parties. The information includes disclosures about a firm's profits, cash flows, assets, and obligations. The interested parties are numerous and include employees, customers, the government, communities, lenders, and investors.

In the United States, Financial Accounting is overseen by a governmental commission, called the ◀**Securities and Exchange Commission (SEC)**▶, located in Washington, D.C. The SEC's role is to ensure that a firm communicates relevant information via Financial Accounting, as it states below:

> *The laws and rules that govern the securities industry in the United States derive from a simple and straightforward concept: all investors, whether large institutions or private individuals, should have access to certain basic facts about an investment prior to buying it.* (**from: www.sec.gov**)

In this book, we will focus on the information needs of lenders and investors. Lenders and investors need financial information to assess a firm's past results and to make predictions about future results. They make these assessments and predictions in order to decide whether to lend to, or invest in, a firm. ◀**Lenders**▶ are also called debtholders, bondholders, or more generally, creditors. ◀**Investors**▶ are also called stockholders, shareholders, equity holders, or more generally, owners.

What do lenders and investors want in return for their loans and investments? Lenders want to be paid back the amount loaned, plus interest, and investors want their investments to increase in value and possibly to receive a dividend.

Why do firms need the cash from these outside sources? Firms need the cash, especially as they are just getting started, in order to fund their businesses. Firms need to buy buildings, supplies, and inventory. They need to hire employees. They must advertise their products and services to customers. All of these require cash.

Lenders and investors are providers of "private capital," as opposed to "public capital," which is cash from the government (or taxpayers). Providers of private capital seek investment opportunities for economic reasons, meaning that they try to identify those firms that are expected to provide the returns that the lenders and investors require. Private capital identifies firms that are likely to create, invent, and produce products and services that people want to buy. True, private capital can make mistakes, but Financial Accounting provides information that helps assess the risks and rewards before making a lending or investing decision. When private capital makes a bad decision, it suffers the consequences.

A WORD ON TERMINOLOGY

Broadly speaking, "capital" is how firms fund the business. New capital is typically an injection of cash into the firm.

Lenders and investors monitor firms' decisions, and they try to protect their interests. Lenders can include restrictions on firms in their lending contracts. That is, lenders can limit what firms do with the borrowed money. Similarly, because investors have the right to vote, they can vote for new managers and directors, if they so choose. These actions provide powerful incentives and discipline on corporate behavior. Arguably, public capital will not keep the same disciplinary focus on firms because the lending and investing decisions are made for political reasons, and politicians may have different goals in mind, rather than the goals of earning sufficient returns on loans and investments.

Part of the SEC's charge, in addition to making sure that firms provide relevant financial information, is to regulate the markets and impose fines on firms who "break the rules." In the extreme, when managers intentionally mislead suppliers of capital, they commit fraud, which is a crime. For instance, a firm may intentionally misreport financial results in order to keep the stock price high. Managers, who may own some of the stock, could sell their shares before the fraud comes to light. The temptation to undertake actions that benefit certain constituencies at the expense of others is an ongoing problem that must constantly be monitored, regardless of whether the main suppliers of capital are public or private.

The U.S. Congress passed a law in 2002, known as ◀**Sarbanes-Oxley (or "SOX"** for short)▶, that requires the Chief Executive Officer (CEO) and the Chief Financial Officer (CFO) to certify their Financial Statements. The certification states that the Financial Statements, based on the CEO's and CFO's knowledge, do "not contain any untrue statement of a material fact or omit to state a material fact necessary to make the statements...not misleading" (excerpted from Lowe's Corporation, 2008 financial report). The wave of corporate frauds in the early 2000s was of such magnitude that the U.S. Congress enacted this and other laws to give the SEC more tools to protect private capital. If private capital loses faith in the integrity of the financial reports, it will not provide the capital that firms need to run their businesses. Thus, Financial Accounting is a critical part of the economy. Major decisions are made on "the numbers," which come from the accounting process.

ASK THE ACCOUNTING GURU

The U.S. government designed SOX, in part, to make Financial Statements more transparent and reliable to the interested parties using the information.

After firms receive outside capital, they convert it to other assets, such as inventory. Then, they execute their business plan by selling the inventory, and they collect cash from customers. Cash from customers is "internally generated capital" from the firm's operations. Firms must sell their products and services at selling prices that are (on average) higher than the cost of the product or service. This will allow the firm not only to pay employees and outside sources of capital, but also to have enough left over to re-invest in the business to create new and improved products and services and to make the business more efficient. If firms do not continuously improve, they will lose to competition.

FINANCIAL ACCOUNTING FOR PRIVATE SECTOR, FOR-PROFIT, PUBLICLY TRADED CORPORATIONS

This book relates primarily to Financial Accounting for publicly traded firms, which are firms whose stock and debt are publicly traded on a public securities exchange, such as the ◀New York Stock Exchange▶. These are the firms whose lenders and investors the SEC has the charge to protect.

Below we provide a broader context. Just about any society can be dichotomized into public and private sectors. The "public sector" pertains to governmental activities, which are undertaken for society at large. "Governmental accounting" is a separate branch of accounting that measures and discloses the activities of governments, which are funded through taxes. We do not cover governmental accounting.

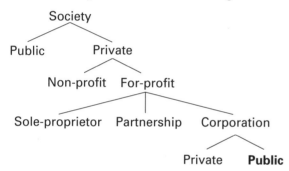

The "private sector" can be split between non-profit and for-profit. Non-profit organizations typically exist for specific humanitarian, educational, or medical purposes. Examples include the Salvation Army and the Rockefeller Foundation. "Fund accounting" measures and discloses the activities of non-profit organizations, which rely mainly on donations. We do not cover fund accounting.

For-profit enterprises include sole-proprietorships, partnerships, and corporations. Sole-proprietorships and partnerships have single and multiple owners, respectively. These two types of enterprises are widespread throughout the economy. They are easy to organize, and they allow the owners to maintain control over their businesses. However, they rarely grow very large because it is difficult for them to access the large amounts of private capital that is often necessary to expand. This is due in part because the owners are often personally liable for the obligations of these businesses. However,

certain limited liability protections are granted to, for example, Limited Liability Companies (LLC) and so-called "S-Corporations." S-Corporations are so-named because the tax requirements fall under Sub-Chapter S of Chapter 1 of the U. S. Internal Revenue Code. Although LLCs and S-Corporations have certain benefits that are not granted to sole-proprietorships, their ownership structures have limits that prevent massive accumulation of capital, thereby typically limiting their size. By comparison, corporations can grow to be quite large as they are able to attract large amounts of capital.

Corporations can be either public or private. As mentioned above, public corporations have stock or debt that is publicly traded on a securities exchange. Private corporations are not publicly traded but are owned by private investors, often referred to as "private equity." = not publically traded

Owners, creditors, employees, and governments want the for-profit firms to earn profits. Profits allow firms to pay higher salaries to employees. Profits allow firms to continue to grow by hiring more employees and investing in new infrastructure and technology. Profits affect stock prices, and investors in public companies want the stock price to rise. Profits also provide the potential to pay dividends to investors. In sum, profits attract private capital.

In conclusion, this book is primarily about corporations. The focus on this select group is driven by the fact that these organizations create significant amounts of wealth that can affect large portions of the economy, government, and society in general. Indeed, the stock market "crash" of 1929, and more recently the Enron and Worldcom debacles, all pointed out the need for transparent reporting of financial information that is measured and recognized according to well-understood accounting standards. Firms must communicate to their constituencies what they have been doing with "other people's money," and how they have performed. As we will see shortly, the accounting model that we use to measure and report firms' financial position is a stewardship model. The assets of the firm are entrusted to managers to manage on behalf of others. Therefore, the managers must report to these various "stakeholders" on a periodic basis, according to agreed upon accounting rules, what they have been doing as stewards.

STANDARD SETTERS AND AUDITORS

In the U.S., the accounting rules are written by the ◀**Financial Accounting Standards Board (FASB)**▶. This organization is under the jurisdiction of the SEC. The SEC has authorized FASB to write the accounting rules that publicly traded corporations must use. The rules of the FASB constitute ◀**GAAP**▶, which is an acronym that stands for "Generally Accepted Accounting Principles." The FASB is located in Norwalk, Connecticut and is headed by Leslie Seidman. Publicly traded firms must file financial reports with the SEC on a periodic basis. By law, the Financial Statements must follow GAAP, and they must be audited by an independent audit firm.

The primary audit firms in the U.S. are referred to as the "Big 4." The Big 4 are Deloitte Touche Tohmatsu, Ernst & Young, KPMG, and PricewaterhouseCoopers. The next tier of audit firms includes J.H. Cohn, McCladrey and Pullen, Grant Thornton, and BDO Seidman, among others. Public accounting firms have to follow professional auditing standards in conducting their audits of publicly held firms. The standards are written by the Public Company Accounting Oversight Board (PCAOB). Their audits of firms will conclude with an "audit opinion," which states that the Financial Statements are the responsibility of management, and that the auditors are responsible for rendering an opinion about whether the Financial Statements "present fairly," in accordance with GAAP, the financial position and results of the firm.

Other nations have their own GAAPs that contrast in varying degrees with U.S. GAAP. A movement is underway to create a single, global accounting language. In particular, the ◀**International Accounting Standards Board (IASB)**▶ has been working to draft a set of rules that will be used trans-nationally in order to facilitate comparisons between and among firms in different countries. Many nations have already adopted IASB GAAP, and the U.S. may one day also adopt these standards. In fact, the SEC has proposed requiring certain large U.S. firms to convert to IASB GAAP by 2015.

> **TIPS OF THE TRADE**
>
> IASB GAAP is commonly referred to as International Financial Reporting Standards (IFRS). There are many GAAPs in the world – IASB and U.S. GAAP are the two most common GAAPs for publicly traded firms.

As we go through the text, we will see some accounting rules that do not seem to make sense. It is good to remind ourselves that standard setting follows a "due process." Anyone can participate in the process by letting his or her opinions be known. For instance, the FASB will issue an "Exposure Draft" of a proposed new rule and ask for comments during a "comment period." The FASB will then deliberate and take under consideration the various comments. The final standard therefore may reflect the varied interests of many different constituencies that would be affected by the new standard. Thus, some rules just will not make sense, unless we consider how the rules became rules and read the comment letters. We sometimes say that our standards do not come down from a "mountaintop," but rather from Connecticut, meaning that our standards were written by mortals, doing the best that they (we) can under current circumstances and practical constraints. When rules do not make sense, users of financial information are free to adjust the Financial Statements to suit their own purposes. We will introduce a few of these techniques at appropriate points in the text.

FASB writes GAAP

IASB = intl version of GAAP

BASIC TERMINOLOGY AND METHODOLOGY

The Fundamental Accounting Equation

The below equation is called the "fundamental accounting equation:"

Assets = Liabilities + Owners' Equity

The equation shows the Assets that a firm has, and it shows the sources of the Assets. Assets include, for example, cash, inventory, and buildings. The capital required to purchase assets comes from creditors and owners. Stated alternatively, Liabilities and Owners' Equity represent, respectively, creditor and investor claims on the assets.

Understanding accounting allows us to understand more clearly the economics of a firm, namely how a firm has employed scarce resources (including financial capital) and whether it was successful in doing so. Accounting also helps us predict what firms will do next, how they will perform in the future, and how risky they will be. The fundamental accounting equation is central to the assessments of past performance, as well as predictions of future performance and risk.

Even though accounting facilitates understanding the economics of a firm, virtually all accounting systems fail in some measure to capture a firm's total economic picture. For example, arguably, firms' most valuable assets are their employees, yet accounting systems rarely measure the value of people and classify their value as assets. As another example, certain debt arrangements are not included among the liabilities of a firm, even though they represent real economic liabilities.

off balance sheet

Accounting falls short for a number of reasons, which we will discuss at various points in the text, and we will show what adjustments are commonly made to overcome these shortcomings. Also, the SEC, aware of these deficiencies, constantly pushes the FASB to improve accounting standards. However, while the FASB deliberates and goes through the due process of adopting new standards, the SEC often requires disclosures in other ways to let lenders and investors have the relevant information, even though it may not be captured in the fundamental accounting equation. Disclosures not captured in the fundamental accounting equation are called ◀note disclosures.▶

A WORD ON TERMINOLOGY

Besides "notes disclosures," other names that you may run across are: footnotes, notes, details, supporting information and disclosures.

Managers undertake actions that change their firms' fundamental equation. We will record the changes directly in the equation by simply writing pluses (+) and minuses (-) in the appropriate columns, as illustrated below.

Let's record a series of numbered transactions for a firm that is just getting started. Assume that the firm decides to borrow $100 in cash from a bank. This would be recorded as follows.

1. Borrow $100 cash.

Assets	Liabilities	Owners' Equity
100 Cash	100 Note Payable	

Assets increase by $100 and liabilities increase by $100. The asset account involved in the transaction is Cash and the liability account is "Note Payable." The names of accounts are generally not standardized. For instance, instead of "Note Payable," firms may use "Bank Debt," or some other similarly descriptive account title.

Assume that the firm needs more cash, and it decides to sell stock to investors, rather than borrow from the bank. The first sale of stock to public investors is called the ◀Initial Public Offering (or IPO)▶. Later, if it decides to sell more stock publicly, these subsequent sales are called ◀Seasoned Equity Offerings (or SEO)▶. Suppose it sells stock valued at $100. This would be recorded as follows:

SEO = sales after IPO

2. Sell stock to investors for $100 cash.

Assets	Liabilities	Owners' Equity
100 Cash		100 Stock

In this case, the $100 of cash is shown as coming from investors.

So, the firm has $200 in cash, half from debt and half from equity. Managers are not hired to obtain cash and stuff it under the mattress. Rather, they must make a decision about what to do with the cash in order to generate returns for the providers of capital. This decision will be based upon a business plan, a strategy, a vision, etc. Let's say the firm decides initially to use $80 of its cash to buy a building. We would write the following:

3. Buy a building for $80 cash.

Assets	Liabilities	Owners' Equity
(80) Cash		
80 Building		

Cash is reduced by $80. Building (an asset) replaces the cash.

Now, let's assume that management decides to use $40 of its cash to buy inventory. This would be booked as follows.

4. Buy inventory for $40 cash.

Assets	Liabilities	Owners' Equity
(40) Cash		
40 Inventory		

Cash is reduced by $40, and inventory (an asset) is increased by $40.

◄Journal Entries►

The four panels above are journal entries. Journal entries give changes (+ and -) in the fundamental accounting equation. They record both sides of a transaction; thus, they always have at least two parts. This system is called the double-entry system, developed in 1494 in Venice by an Italian monk, Friar Luca Pacioli, a friend of Leonardo da Vinci. His work, Summa de Arithmetica, Geometria, Proportioni et Proportionalita, although perhaps not a best seller, has certainly had staying-power. We still use the double-entry system centuries later.

TIPS OF THE TRADE

When balancing the fundamental accounting equation try to think to yourself "what is the offset" to make the equation come back into parity. In other words, what must be added / subtracted as an "offset" to make the equation balance.

Journal entries are recorded in the "journal," which is a sort of financial diary. The journal is also called the "book of original entry." The journal contains the data about the transactions that eventually "roll up" to the Financial Statements that are presented to lenders and investors.

The above types of journal entries are intuitive, showing the main effects of accounting events on the fundamental accounting equation. Journal entries can be written in an alternative way, using "debits" and "credits." This latter method is conventional. In an upcoming section, we will compare the two methods.

◄The Ledger►

The data from the journal entries are "posted" to individual accounts (Cash, Debt, Stock, etc.) to accumulate the account balances. The account balances are stored in the ledger. The table below is our ledger for this firm at this point in time.

	Assets	Cash	Inventory	Building	Total Assets	Liabilities	Note Payable	Owners' Equity	Stock	Total Liabilities & Owners' Equity
Begin		0	0	0	**0**		0		0	**0**
1		100					100			
2		100							100	
3		(80)		80						
4		(40)	40							
End		80	40	80	**200**		100		100	**200**

(Event Numbers label the rows 1–4)

The beginning balances are in the top row, increases and decreases to the balances are in the rows numbered 1–4, and then the ending balances are in the last row. In this example, the beginning balances are all zero, because the firm is just commencing its business.

◄Balance Sheet►

The Balance Sheet is a listing of the balances from the ledger. As the name suggests, it shows the balances at a point in time. The "Begin" and "End" rows above (in the ledger) would represent this firm's consecutive Balance Sheets.

Now assume that the firm sells half of its inventory ($20) for $80 in cash. In this transaction, we have two pairs of accounts to track. In fact, all sales of inventory have this characteristic. One pair of accounts shows the sale and the inflow of cash. The other shows the cost of the products sold and the outflow of inventory. The events would be recorded as follows, with explanation below.

5. Sell half of the inventory for $80 cash.

Assets	Liabilities	Owners' Equity
80 Cash		80 Revenues
(20) Inventory		(20) Cost of Goods Sold

Notice how ◄**Revenues**▶ (also called Sales) are recorded as increases in Owners' Equity and that ◄**Cost of Goods Sold**▶ is recorded as a reduction in Owners' Equity. Cost of Goods Sold is an expense. It corresponds to the reduction in inventory that was necessary to generate the revenue. Without the inventory, there would have been no sale. (Cost of Goods Sold is usually abbreviated CGS or COGS.)

More generally, expenses are necessary to generate revenues. Expenses generate, either directly or indirectly, a sale, and they must be recognized during the period when the sale is recognized. We are reminded of the expression, "You have to spend money to make money." In fact, in accounting, if a firm is booking sales, it must be booking related expenses. A firm cannot show sales without showing expenses.

A WORD ON TERMINOLOGY

"Booking" is the act of recording any event or transaction in the firm's financial system.

Revenues are credited to the owners of the firm, and expenses are charged to the owners. This is why we put the revenues and expense in the Owners' Equity column. Also, revenues and expenses are reflected in a firm's ◄**Income Statement**▶. As we will see, the Income Statement becomes part of Owners' Equity.

The difference between Revenues and Cost of Goods Sold is the profit on the sale ($60). More commonly, this amount is called ◄**Gross Profit**▶ or "Gross Margin."

Now let's assume that the firm pays wages to its employees. Assume it pays $10 cash. This would be recorded in the following way:

6. Pay wages of $10 cash.

Assets	Liabilities	Owners' Equity
(10) Cash		(10) Wage Expense

Wage Expense is also necessary to generate sales. The firm needs employees to serve customers and without the service, there may not have been a sale.

Both Cost of Goods Sold and Wage Expense are expenses and will be deducted from revenues in order to measure the firm's ◄**Net Income.**▶

In sum, revenues are credited to the owners by adding them to Owners' Equity, and expenses are charged against the owners by subtracting them from Owners' Equity. Alternatively stated, Net Income, which combines all revenues and expenses, accrues to the owners of the firm.

A BIT OF PERSPECTIVE

Net Income is a calculation over a period of time and is shown on the Income Statement.

Let's consider a few more expenses, and then we'll measure Net Income.

Earlier the firm bought a building. The firm recorded the building as an asset. However, as the firm uses the building, it must ◄**depreciate**▶ the building. This means that the building account is reduced systematically over its expected life. Assume the expected life is 4 years. Thus, the firm will "expense" one-fourth of the building, or $20. This would be recorded as follows:

7. Depreciate the building by $20.

Assets	Liabilities	Owners' Equity
(20) Building		(20) Depreciation Expense

Depreciation Expense is another expense. The building is necessary to conduct business (to make sales), so part of the building is reduced and "expensed" each period over which the firm receives benefits from using it.

Earlier the firm borrowed money from the bank. The fee charged by the bank for the use of the borrowed funds is interest, and it must be recognized as another expense in the periods during which the firm used the borrowed money. Assume that it owes the bank $10 in interest on the amount borrowed. Assume, however, that it does not have to pay the bank on this date, but rather, it will pay the interest in the future. The journal entry would look like this:

8. Book $10 of interest expense to be paid later.

Assets	Liabilities	Owners' Equity
	10 Interest Payable	(10) Interest Expense

The expense must be booked in the current period, because the firm had the borrowed money (and benefitted from having it during the current period) regardless of the fact that the firm does not pay cash for the interest in the current period. Thus, to balance the entry, the firm records "Interest Payable," indicating that it owes $10 to the bank and that it will pay it in the future.

Finally, the firm has to calculate what it owes the government for taxes. Taxes are calculated as a percentage of taxable income. The percentage is called the tax rate. In the U.S., the tax rate on corporations is currently 35%. Let's calculate taxable income by assuming that the above sale and all the expenses correspond exactly to what the government has determined through its tax law to be taxable items and deductible items, respectively. Tax Expense, calculated below, is another expense of doing business.

Tax Expense = Pre-Tax Income x Tax Rate
Revenues $80
Cost of Goods Sold.. (20)
Wage Expense .... (10)
Depreciation Expense.................................... (20)
Interest Expense .... (10)
Pre-Tax Income.. 20
Tax Expense (35% x $20) .... (7)

Let's assume that the firm is not going to pay the tax on this date, but rather at some future time. The firm would book Tax Expense in the following way.

9. Book $7 of Tax Expense to be paid later.

Assets	Liabilities	Owners' Equity
	7 Taxes Payable	(7) Tax Expense

After booking tax expense, the firm then knows its Net Income, which is the difference between its revenues and all of its expenses. The revenues and expenses are listed on the Income Statement, shown below:

Income Statement

Revenues	$80
Cost of Goods Sold...	(20)
Wage Expense	(10)
Depreciation Expense..	(20)
Interest Expense	(10)
Pre-Tax Income..	20
Tax Expense	(7)
Net Income...	13

A WORD ON TERMINOLOGY

Besides "Revenues" other names you may come across in Financial Statements are "Sales" and "Turnover". Outside of Financial Statements in more casual discussions, "Revenues" are often referred to as the "top-line" (referring to the top line on the Income Statement) and are a common reference to the size of a firm. For example, "a three billion firm" had three billion in Revenues for the most recent year—a three billion "top-line".

Now we are ready to take another picture of this company and show the updated account balances in the ledger. We also have a few new accounts to add to the ledger, namely Interest Payable, Taxes Payable, and Retained Earnings. **(See Exhibit 1.1)**

$A = L + E$

EXHIBIT 1.1

		Assets				Liabilities					Owners' Equity				
		Cash	Inventory	Building	Total Assets		Note Payable	Interest Payable	Taxes Payable	Total Liabilities		Stock	Retained Earnings	Total Owners' Equity	Total Liabilities & Owners' Equity
Begin		0	0	0	**0**		0	0	0	**0**		0	0	**0**	**0**
Event Numbers	1	100					100								
	2	100										100			
	3	(80)		80											
	4	(40)	40												
	5	80											80		
	5		(20)										(20)		
	6	(10)											(10)		
	7			(20)									(20)		
	8							10					(10)		
	9								7				(7)		
End		150	20	60	**230**		100	10	7	**117**		100	13	**113**	**230**

The fundamental equation (Assets = Liabilities + Owners' Equity) balances: 230 = 117 + 113.

Let's now describe one of the new accounts that appears above.

◄Retained Earnings►

Retained Earnings is an account on the Balance Sheet that collects all of the revenues and expenses of the firm. In the journal entries, we simply put revenues and expenses in the Owners' Equity column, but they end up in Retained Earnings, as we can see above. Next year, the firm will add the revenues and expenses for that year to the above balance of Retained Earnings. Thus, Retained Earnings is the cumulative amount of Net Income that the firm has earned since its inception. Since this is the first year of operations for this firm, the balance in Retained Earnings ($13) exactly equals the Net Income for this year. All of the changes in the Retained Earnings account (+80-20-10-20-10-7) correspond to the individual items on the Income Statement.

Later, we will introduce one more adjustment to Retained Earnings, namely dividends. Whenever a firm decides to pay a dividend to its owners, Retained Earnings are reduced. This is why it is called Retained Earnings. These are the cumulative earnings of the firm that are not paid out as dividends to owners.

ASK THE ACCOUNTING GURU

The Balance Sheet, Income Statement and Statement of Cash Flows are a firm's primary statements. Another statement that you may see is the Statement of Owners' Equity. These statements, when combined with the firm's note disclosures are collectively referred to as the firm's "Financial Statements".

‹Statement of Cash Flows›

In addition to the Balance Sheet and the Income Statement, a final statement that we will study is the Statement of Cash Flows. The Statement of Cash Flows shows the cash into and the cash out of the firm. Under accounting rules, the cash flows must be classified. The categories are:

1. operating cash flows—from customers and to suppliers

2. investing cash flows—for purchases of buildings and some other items

3. financing cash flows—to and from lenders and investors

If we take the cash account from the ledger above and label the cash flows, we will have the Statement of Cash Flows. Below we have isolated the cash account from the ledger, and we have added some explanatory labels. **(See Exhibit 1.2)**

EXHIBIT 1.2

		Cash	Event	Cash Category
Begin		0		
Event Numbers	1	100	Debt	Financing
	2	100	Stock	Financing
	3	(80)	Building	Investing
	4	(40)	Inventory	Operating
	5	80	Sales	Operating
	6	(10)	Wages	Operating
End		150		

Raising capital from lenders and investors is a "financing" activity. Therefore, the cash received in the first two transactions would be "financing cash flows." Then, $80 of cash was spent on the building. Cash spent on buildings is classified as an "investing cash flow." (More generally, cash spent on buildings and other property is called ‹capital expenditures,› or "capex" for short.) The purchase of inventory is classified as an "operating cash flow," because inventory is directly used in the operations of the business. Similarly, the cash received from the sale and the wages paid to employees are both operating cash flows, because they, too, correspond to the

operating activities of the firm. We will spend a good deal of time in future chapters classifying many different types of cash flows.

Below, the above cash flows are aggregated by type to form the Statement of Cash Flows. The Statement of Cash Flows always ends with a reconciliation of the beginning cash balance to the ending cash balance.

Statement of Cash Flows

Cash from Operating Activities (-40+80-10)	30
Cash used in Investing Activities (-80)	(80)
Cash from Financing Activities (+100+100)	200
Total Change in Cash	150
Beginning Cash Balance	0
Ending Cash Balance	150

The Statement of Cash Flows, therefore, explains the change in the cash balance. It went from a balance of $0 to a balance of $150. The firm generated $30 of cash from its central operations (buying and selling inventory and paying wages). It used $80 in investing activities (buying the building), and it received $200 from financing activities (raising capital from lenders and investors).

Notice that the Income Statement shows Net Income of $13. This equals the change in Retained Earnings in the ledger and on the Balance Sheet. Specifically, Retained Earnings started with a balance of $0 and ended with $13, which equals the amount of Net Income for the period. This feature of interrelated Financial Statements is referred to as "articulation." The Income Statement articulates with Retained Earnings, and the Statement of Cash Flows articulates with the cash account.

Below, we present the three primary Financial Statements.

We point out the "dates," namely the fact that the Balance Sheet is reported "as of" a particular point in time and the Income Statement and the Statement of Cash Flows are reported "for a period of time." The reasons are because the Balance Sheet is a cumulative statement (a summation of events at a particular point in time), whereas the other two statements contain results over a reporting period, either one year or quarter. Also, below, we expand the Statement of Cash Flows to give some additional detail.

Balance Sheet
As of the End of the First Year of Operations

Assets

Cash	150
Inventory	20
Building	60
Total Assets	**230**

Liabilities

Note Payable	100
Interest Payable	10
Taxes Payable	7
Total Liabilities	**117**

Owners' Equity

Stock	100
Retained Earnings	13
Total Owners' Equity	113
Total Liabilities & Owners' Equity	**230**

Income Statement
For the First Year of Operations

Revenues	80
Cost of Goods Sold	(20)
Wage Expense	(10)
Depreciation Expense	(20)
Interest Expense	(10)
Taxable Income	20
Tax Expense	(7)
Net Income	**13**

Statement of Cash Flows
For the First Year of Operations

Cash from Operating Activities

Cash received from customers	80
Cash paid to suppliers of inventory	(40)
Cash paid to employees	(10)
Total Cash from Operating Activities	**30**

Cash used in Investing Activities

Capital expenditures	(80)

Cash from Financing Activities

Cash received from the sale of stock	100
Cash received from new borrowing	100
Total Cash from Financing Activities	**200**
Total Change in Cash	150
Beginning Cash Balance	0
Ending Cash Balance	**150**

CLOSING THE BOOKS

There is one more journal entry that we wish to introduce at this point. When we did this example, our ledger did not include the Income Statement accounts. However, the ledger contains all accounts, both for the Balance Sheet and for the Income Statement. After all, if we need to know total sales for a period of time, we would look at the ledger.

Therefore, rather than placing sales and all of the expenses directly in Retained Earnings (as we did before), we first place them in their respective accounts. This brings us to the new journal entry. It is called the ◀closing entry.▶

The purpose of the closing entry is to re-set the balances in the revenue and expense accounts to zero so that they can accumulate the next period's revenues and expenses. That is, revenues and expenses are accumulated over each reporting period. For example, we speak of revenues and expenses for the period (year or quarter) and Net Income for the period. Each revenue and expense account has its own ledger account, just as all Balance Sheet accounts do. However, revenues and expenses hold their account balances temporarily. In fact, they are called ◀temporary accounts.▶ They are closed at the end of each accounting period. This is accomplished by transferring their balances to Retained Earnings. The closing entry would be the final journal entry and is shown below.

- -
A BIT OF PERSPECTIVE

Closing the books is an accounting process performed by a firm's accountants as part of producing Financial Statements. This process is also important to users of financial statements (you!) because it links the Balance Sheet, Income Statement and Cash Flows Statements together which is a key to understanding finance tools such as "Three Statement" financial modeling.
- -

10. The firm closes all temporary accounts.

Assets	Liabilities	Owners' Equity
		(80) Revenue
		20 COGS
		10 Wage Expense
		20 Depreciation Expense
		10 Interest Expense
		7 Tax Expense
		13 Retained Earnings

As we can see, the closing entry simply reverses the signs of all of the revenue and expense accounts. This results in re-setting these temporary account balances to zero and in transferring the net amount, which corresponds to Net Income, to Retained Earnings. Note that the sum of -80, 20, 10, 20, 10, and 7 is minus 13. This amount is offset by a plus 13 to Retained Earnings (in order to balance the fundamental accounting equation). In this way, the temporary accounts are closed and their balances are transferred as a net amount to Retained Earnings.

Below is the new ledger that includes the temporary accounts. The closing entry has been added (event 10). **(See Exhibit 1.3)**

EXHIBIT 1.3

Event Numbers	Cash	Inventory	Building	Total Assets	Note Payable	Interest Payable	Taxes Payable	Total Liabilities	Stock	Retained Earnings	Total Owners' Equity	Revenue	Cost of Goods Sold	Wage Expense	Depreciation Expense	Interest Expense	Tax Expense
Begin	0	0	0	0	0	0	0	0	0	0	0						
1	100				100												
2	100								100								
3	(80)		80														
4	(40)	40															
5	80											80					
5		(20)											(20)				
6	(10)													(10)			
7			(20)												(20)		
8						10										(10)	
9							7										(7)
10										13		(80)	20	10	20	10	7
End	150	20	60	230	100	10	7	117	100	13	113	0	0	0	0	0	0

Chapter 2: Additional Terminology, Concepts, and Methodology

◄THE ACCOUNTING CYCLE►

Firms must report their financial results quarterly. This means that they go through the so-called "Accounting Cycle" quarterly. The accounting cycle has four basic steps, outlined below.

1. The **identification** of accounting events. Accounting events are all events that firms are required to disclose under the accounting rules. The disclosures are made either in the Financial Statements or in the notes to the Financial Statements. Respectively, these are called "statement disclosures" and "note disclosures." Both are important sources of information.

2. The **valuation** of accounting events. Firms must measure the events by putting a monetary value on them, if possible.

3. The **recording** of accounting events. Firms must formally record events in the accounting system so that they will be properly disclosed. Recording means that the firm either journalizes the event or provides a note disclosure, depending upon whether the event requires statement recognition (in which case the event is journalized) or note disclosure.

4. The **disclosure** of accounting events. Firms must generate a set of Financial Statements, along with the required note disclosures.

example
By way of review, below we give another example of the accounting cycle. Below are the events and transactions for a firm's first year of operations. We also provide the journal entries. Explanations follow the journal entries.

1. The firm issues $100 in stock for cash.

Assets	Liabilities	Owners' Equity
100 Cash		100 Stock

2. The firm borrows $10 from the bank by issuing a long-term note.

Assets	Liabilities	Owners' Equity
10 Cash	10 Note Payable	

3. The firm buys property, plant, and equipment (PP&E) for $40 by paying $15 in cash and issuing a long-term note for the balance.

Assets	Liabilities	Owners' Equity
40 PP&E	25 Note Payable	
(15) Cash		

4. The firm buys inventory for $20 on credit. A/P stands for Accounts Payable.

Assets	Liabilities	Owners' Equity
20 Inventory	20 A/P	

5. The firm sells $15 of the inventory for $28 in a credit sale. A/R stands for Accounts Receivable.

Assets	Liabilities	Owners' Equity
28 A/R		28 Sales
(15) Inventory		(15) Cost of Goods Sold

6. The firm collects one-half of the receivable booked in event 5.

Assets	Liabilities	Owners' Equity
14 Cash		
(14) A/R		

7. The firm pays $10 to suppliers of inventory that was purchased in 4.

Assets	Liabilities	Owners' Equity
(10) Cash	(10) A/P	

8. The firm records wage expense for $3, which will be paid at a later date.

Assets	Liabilities	Owners' Equity
	3 Wages Payable	(3) Wage Expense

9. The firm records $2 of depreciation expense on the PP&E. A/D stands for Accumulated Depreciation. This is a special account used to record depreciation. It is explained after all the journal entries.

Assets	Liabilities	Owners' Equity
(2) Accumulated Depreciation		(2) Depreciation Expense

10. The firm records interest expense on both notes (events 2 and 3) of $3, which will be paid at a later date.

Assets	Liabilities	Owners' Equity
	3 Interest Payable	(3) Interest Expense

11. The firm records tax expense which will be paid at a later date. The tax rate is assumed to be 40%. The amount of the expense is $2, which is 40% of pre-tax income of $5. Pre-tax income is shown below:

Sales	$28
Cost of Goods Sold	(15)
Wage Expense	(3)
Depreciation Expense	(2)
Interest Expense	(3)
Pre-Tax Income	5

Assets	Liabilities	Owners' Equity
	2 Tax Payable	(2) Tax Expense

In **Event 1**, cash increases by $100. The double-entry system tracks the source of the money (investors). Investors are given stock certificates as evidence of their ownership in the firm. Stock is an account in Owners' Equity. So, for **Event 1**, Assets (cash) and Owners' Equity (stock) both increase by equal amounts.

For **Event 2**, Cash and Note Payable increase.

Event 3 involves an increase to an asset (Property, Plant, & Equipment), a decrease to an asset (Cash), and an increase to a liability (Note Payable).

Events 4, 5, 6, and **7** are connected. Jointly, they make up a regular part of the business cycle. Inventory is purchased (on credit) and sold (on credit). Then, cash is collected, and some of the cash is then remitted to the suppliers of inventory.

Event 8 represents the benefit of labor, which will be paid later.

Events 9 and **10** are so-called "adjusting entries." Adjusting entries update account balances. They are typically a function of time and do not involve cash. Adjusting entries are made at the end of the period, right before the closing entry.

In **Event 9**, we record depreciation expense. In an earlier section, when we booked depreciation expense, we reduced the depreciable asset directly for ease of presentation. Firms, however, do not reduce the PP&E account directly. Rather, they use an account called "Accumulated Depreciation," (A/D) which is subtracted from the PP&E account. Accumulated Depreciation is a called a "contra-account." Its purpose is to let investors know approximately how old the PP&E is, as measured by the amount of depreciation that has been recorded. For instance, in this case, the firm has $2 of Accumulated Depreciation on the PP&E that costs $40. Thus, the PP&E is only 5% depreciated (2/40 = 5%). Going forward, we will use the contra-account.

Event 10 represents interest expense required on the use of borrowed funds.

Event 11 represents accrued tax expense that will be paid later.

As before, at the end of the period, the temporary accounts, which are all of the Income Statement accounts, are closed to Retained Earnings. All of the temporary accounts' signs are simply reversed. That is, sales are negative and expenses are positive. We label this as *Event 12*.

12. The firm makes the closing entry

Assets	Liabilities	Owners' Equity
		(28) Sales
		15 Cost of Goods Sold
		3 Wage Expense
		2 Depreciation Expense
		3 Interest Expense
		2 Tax Expense
		3 Retained Earnings

Below, all of the journal entries are posted to the ledger. **(see exhibit 2.1)**

As mentioned previously, the Statement of Cash Flows simply explains how the firm's cash balance changed from the beginning of the period to the end. The cash flows are grouped into three categories:

- *Cash from Operating Activities*
- *Cash from Investing Activities*
- *Cash from Financing Activities*

The classification into the three categories is usually self-evident. The cash coming into the firm in events 1 and 2 are financing cash flows ($100 + $10). The cash going out of the firm in event 3 is an investing cash flow (-$15). The remaining cash flows identified in events 6 (+$14) and 7 (-$10) are operating cash flows. Therefore, the firm goes from a cash balance of zero to a cash balance of $99 (99 = 100 + 10 − 15 + 14 − 10).

EXHIBIT 2.1

Event	Assets	Cash	Accounts Receivable	Inventory	Building	Accumulated Depreciation	Total Assets	Liabilities	Accounts Payable	Wages Payable	Interest Payable	Taxes Payable	Note Payable	Total Liabilities	Owners' Equity	Stock	Retained Earnings	Total Owners' Equity	Total Liabilities & Owners' Equity	Sales	Cost of Goods Sold	Wage Expense	Depreciation Expense	Interest Expense	Tax Expense
Begin		0	0	0	0	0	**0**		0	0	0	0	0	**0**		0	0	**0**	**0**						
1		100														100									
2		10											10												
3		(15)			40								25												
4				20					20																
5			28																	28					
5				(15)																	(15)				
6		14	(14)																						
7		(10)							(10)																
8										3												(3)			
9						(2)																	(2)		
10											3													(3)	
11												2													(2)
12																	3			(28)	15	3	2	3	2
End		99	14	5	40	(2)	**156**		10	3	3	2	35	**53**		100	3	**103**	**156**	0	0	0	0	0	0

In sum, the accounting cycle is:

1. *The identification of accounting events*

2. *The valuation of accounting events*

3. *The recording of accounting events*

4. *The disclosure of accounting events, both in the Financial Statements and in the notes.*

The statements in this simple example would be as follows:

Company Name
Balance Sheet at December 31, X

Assets

Current Assets

Cash	$99
Accounts Receivable	14
Inventory	5
Total Current Assets	**118**

Non-Current Assets

Property, Plant & Equipment	40
Accumulated Depreciation	(2)
Net Property Plant & Equipment	38
Total Assets	**$156**

Liabilities

Current Liabilities

Accounts Payable	$10
Wages Payable	3
Interest Payable	3
Tax Payable	2
Total Current Liabilities	**18**

Non-Current Liabilities

Note Payable	35
Total Liabilities	**$53**

Owners' Equity

Stock	$100
Retained Earnings	3
Total Owners' Equity	$103
Total Liabilities & Owners' Equity	**$156**

Company Name
Income Statement for the period ended December 31, X

Sales	$28
Cost of Goods Sold	(15)
Wage Expense	(3)
Depreciation Expense	(2)
Interest Expense	(3)
Tax Expense	(2)
Net Income	3

Statement of Cash Flows
For the period ended December 31, X

Cash from Operating Activities

Cash received from customers	14
Cash paid to suppliers of inventory	(10)
Total Cash from Operating Activities	**4**

Cash used in Investing Activities

Capital expenditures	(15)

Cash from Financing Activities

Cash received from the sale of stock	100
Cash received from new borrowing	10
Total Cash from Financing Activities	**110**

Total Change in Cash	99
Beginning Cash Balance	0
Ending Cash Balance	**99**

TIPS OF THE TRADE

The "current" classifications on a balance sheet usually imply that the current asset will be converted to cash or the or current liability will be paid with cash within one year. This is important to users of Financial Statements when analyzing a firm's ability to satisfy its obligations to pay cash to employees, vendors and capital providers. Much more on this later!

Now that we've had another round of the accounting cycle, let's now turn to some important terminology that we will frequently hear, beginning with capitalize and expense.

CAPITALIZE VERSUS EXPENSE

🔥 ◀**Capitalize**▶ means that an asset increases.

🔥 ◀**Expense**▶ means that Owners' Equity decreases.

Capitalize and expense can be considered antonyms.

Assume that a firm spends $10 to buy a pencil sharpener. To capitalize the pencil sharpener, the firm would make the following journal entry:

Assets	Liabilities	Owners' Equity
(10) Cash		
10 Office Equipment		

To expense the pencil sharpener, the firm would do the following:

Assets	Liabilities	Owners' Equity
(10) Cash		(10) Office Expense

In both of the above instances, cash is reduced by $10. However, in the first instance, an asset account is increased to offset the decrease in cash. In the second instance, Owners' Equity is decreased to offset the decrease in cash.

When the pencil sharpener is capitalized, one asset is replaced by another (office equipment for cash).

When the pencil sharpener is expensed, both Assets and Owners' Equity are decreased. The Owners' Equity account is "Office Expense." By way of semantics, we say that the effect of the expense is a reduction in Owners' Equity, or we say that the expense is charged against the owners.

Notice that when the pencil sharpener is capitalized (the first instance above) the **net** effect on the firm is zero. The firm's equation (Assets = Liabilities + Owners' Equity) is unchanged. When the pencil sharpener is expensed, the firms "shrinks," as both sides of the equation are reduced by $10.

If the pencil sharpener is capitalized, it will be expensed later, over time, in a systematic way, via the process of depreciation.

Firms do not usually have a choice about whether to capitalize or expense an expenditure. Rather, they must follow GAAP, specifically the definitions of assets and expenses. Assets are probable future benefits, extending beyond the current reporting period, say 1 year. Does a pencil sharpener provide future benefits extending beyond the current year?

Can one depreciate an expense? No? (handwritten note)

Strictly speaking, yes. If the firm capitalizes the asset, it would then have to depreciate the asset over its expected useful life. For instance, if the pencil sharpener were expected to last for, say, 5 years, then the firm would take $2 per year ($10 cost / 5 years) over five years from column 1 (Assets) and column 3 (Owners' Equity). This particular depreciation schedule is called "straight-line" since an equal amount of depreciation is recorded each year.

The journal entry would be booked as follows:

Assets	Liabilities	Owners' Equity
(2) Accumulated Depreciation		(2) Depreciation Expense

Even though the pencil sharpener is strictly speaking an asset, accounting does have a materiality threshold which allows for some discretion or judgment. A $10 expenditure, in the scheme of all accounting transactions, may be considered immaterial. Therefore the firm may go ahead and expense the pencil sharpener in the period of purchase, rather than going through the laborious exercise of capitalizing the pencil sharpener and expensing it (through depreciation) over the ensuing 5 years.

However, many firms have been accused of "cooking the books" by incorrectly capitalizing items that *should clearly have been expensed* because of their materiality. For instance, a firm called Worldcom was accused of intentionally capitalizing many billions of dollars of items that should have been expensed. Why? Expenses, which reduce Owners' Equity and therefore Net Income, were shifted to an Asset account to make the firm look profitable and to be able to meet so-called "earnings expectations" on Wall Street. Firms do not want to announce unexpected bad news to investors. Investors do not like such surprises. They will typically react to the news by selling the stock, which will drive down the stock price. So, Worldcom, in order to hide the unexpected bad news, capitalized the expense (as depicted below) and misled investors.

Assets =	Liabilities	Owners' Equity
(Cash)		
Asset ◀		(Expense)

What can destroy a firm? Obviously natural disasters can, but fraudulent journal entries can do equal amounts of damage. Lenders and investors lose confidence in the firm and withdraw or withhold capital. Customers flee. Employees are laid off. The business collapses.

Let's look at a few more concepts we will need.

GAINS AND LOSSES VERSUS REVENUES AND EXPENSES

◀Gains▶ are similar to revenues, but they are the result of peripheral activities, which are activities that are not central and ongoing activities of the firm, as in the case of revenues.

example

A firm sells a piece of equipment for $1,000 cash. The firm had used the equipment in its manufacturing process to produce products (inventory) that it sells. Thus, the firm's central, ongoing operation is the production of inventory for resale. The equipment is listed on the firm's Balance Sheet at $800.

The journal entry would be as follows:

Assets		Liabilities	Owners' Equity
1,000	Cash		200 Gain
(800)	Equipment		

If the firm had been in the business of selling the equipment, rather than using the equipment to produce a product, the firm would record the transaction in the following way:

Assets		Liabilities	Owners' Equity	
1,000	Cash		1,000	Revenue
(800)	Equipment		(800)	COGS

Thus, we see that when the firm's central activity is selling a product that the equipment produces, rather than equipment itself, the firm has a gain. Intuitively, the gain is the difference between the fair value of the equipment ($1,000) and its book value listed on the Balance Sheet ($800).

When the firm's central activity is selling equipment, the firm has revenue ($1,000) and an expense (Cost of Goods Sold of $800). Notice that the result of the two different treatments is identical. Assets increase by $200 (net) and Owners' Equity increases by $200 (net). The difference is in the level of detail. Peripheral activities are reported on a "net" basis; central activities are reported as two numbers, or on

a "gross" basis (Revenues less COGS).

◀Losses▶ are similar to expenses, but they result from peripheral activities. Losses are mirror images of gains.

example

Assume the above firm sells the same piece of equipment for $600 cash and that the firm used the equipment in its manufacturing process to produce inventory. The sale of the equipment would be recorded in the following way.

Assets		Liabilities	Owners' Equity	
600	Cash		(200)	Loss
(800)	Equipment			

Here, the firm sells the equipment below book value. That is, the market value of the equipment is $600, but its book value (that is, the value of the equipment shown on the firm's books, or Balance Sheet) is $800.

ASK THE ACCOUNTING GURU

Firms frequently sell equipment and other assets unrelated to their central activity. These sales are almost always for amounts greater than and less than the book value on the Balance Sheet. Users of Financial Statements must use other sources of information outside of the financial statements (such as appraisals and market reports) when analyzing the firm. However, Financial Statements are a great place to start analyzing a firm. Pulling together different pieces of information and putting that information to work is part of the art of Financial Statement Analysis.

One reason for the distinction between revenues and gains and between expenses and losses is to help lenders and investors understand future consequences. Revenues and expenses are more likely to persist because they are central and ongoing. Gains and losses are not as likely to recur. Since making predictions about a firm's financial future is important to lenders and investors, the distinction is critical.

When firms announce their earnings, we always look to see if gains and losses (particularly gains) are imbedded in Net Income. Net Income can sometimes be "propped up" from these largely "one time" boosts. We say that earnings that are more sustainable, that is, which do not include gains and losses, are of "higher quality."

STATUTORY TAX RATES VERSUS EFFECTIVE TAX RATES

In the examples above, we used tax rates of 35% and 40%. These rates, which we simply assumed, are called the statutory rates.

In our examples, the statutory rates also were the same as so-called "Effective Tax Rates," but this is rarely the case in reality.

The Effective Tax Rate is defined as follows:

$$\text{Effective Tax Rate} = \frac{\text{Tax Expense}}{\text{Pre-tax Income}}$$

In the first example, where Pre-tax Income and Tax Expense were $20 and $7, respectively, the ◄**Effective Tax Rate►** would be calculated as follows:

Effective Tax Rate = 7 / 20
= 35%

Similarly, in the second example, where Pre-tax Income and Tax Expense were $5 and $2, respectively, the Effective Tax Rate would be calculated as follows:

Effective Tax Rate = 2 / 5
= 40%

In both cases, the effective rates equaled the assumed ◄**Statutory Rates,►** which are set by a nation's government. Statutory tax Rates vary around the world. Sometimes firms will conduct part of their business in other countries where the tax rate is lower. When a firm uses a mixture of statutory rates, the Effective Tax Rate can differ from the local Statutory Rate.

Not only do statutory rates vary across nations, sometimes within the same country, a government will tax some items at different rates. In fact, some items are not taxed at all, in which case the statutory rate for that particular item is zero. For instance, in the U.S., interest earned on municipal bonds is typically not taxed. Municipal bonds are bonds that are issued by municipalities (cities and towns). The federal government does not tax this interest because it wants to entice investors to loan money to cities and towns who need capital for various public projects. Of course, the nontaxable status of municipal bonds could always change.

example

Assume a firm has the following Income Statement.

Income Statement

Sales	100
Cost of Goods Sold	(60)
Wage Expense	(10)
Depreciation Expense	(2)
Interest Expense	(8)
Pre-Tax Income	20
Tax Expense	(8)
Net Income	**12**

The Effective Tax Rate is calculated below:

Effective Tax Rate = Tax Expense / Pre-Tax Income
= 8 / 20
= 40%

We repeat the Income Statement below but add $5 of Municipal Interest.

Income Statement

Sales	100
Cost of Goods Sold	(60)
Wage Expense	(10)
Depreciation Expense	(2)
Interest Expense	(8)
Municipal Interest	5
Pre-Tax Income	25
Tax Expense	(8)
Net Income	**17**

As we see, Tax Expense does not change, even though Pre-Tax Income increases by $5 from the Municipal Interest.

Tax Expense can be calculated in the following expanded equation to highlight the zero tax rate on the municipal interest.

Tax Expense = 100x40% – 60x40% – 10x40% – 2x40% – 8x40% + 5x0%
= 8

In this case, the Effective Tax Rate will be lower than the Statutory Rate because of the tax free interest.

Effective Tax Rate = Tax Expense / Pre-Tax Income
= 8 / 25
= 32%

We can always calculate a firm's Effective Tax Rate from the above formula. We can also look in the note disclosures to the Financial Statements, where firms provide not only the Effective Tax Rate, but also the reasons why the Effective Tax Rate differs from the Statutory Rate. This is important because when we build a financial model of the firm's future (for purposes of estimating a firm's value) we want to use the Effective Tax Rate to calculate a firm's tax expense. Knowing the reasons for the differences between the two rates can help the analyst decide whether such differences will persist into the future.

Alternative Methods for Capturing Data: Conventional vs. Intuitive Journal Entries and T-Accounts

Throughout this text, we will use "intuitive" journal entries. For example, when a company borrows $50, we will write:

Assets	Liabilities	Owners' Equity
50 Cash	50 Note Payable	

However, "conventional" journal entries use debits and credits. Using the conventional format, the above intuitive journal entry would be written in the following way:

Debit	Credit	Debit	Credit
Cash		50	
	Note Payable		50

Here are the rules for the conventional format:

- ◀*Debits*▶ are on the left, and credits are indented, thus on the right. In our context, _debit simply means left, and_ ◀*Credit*▶ _means right._ Debit does not mean "bad" or "negative" and credit does not mean "good" or "positive."

- There are n_o negative numbers_ with conventional journal entries.

- _Assets increase with debits and decrease with credits._

- _Liabilities and Owners' Equity do the opposite. They increase with credits and decrease with debits._

- _Revenues, since they increase Owners' Equity, are credits._

- _Expenses, since they decrease Owners' Equity, are debits._

Is your head spinning?

Conventional journal entries have been used for a long time and continue to be used. Journal entries are part of bookkeeping, and this is not a text about bookkeeping, but rather about concepts. Although we use many journal entries in this text, we do so to illustrate the effects of managerial decisions (and their related accounting treatment) on the fundamental equation, and these effects are most easily seen with the intuitive method. However, if any reader is thinking about upper level accounting courses or a career in public accounting, conventional journal entries should be practiced.

To add more structure to the instructions for the conventional journal entries, let's put in some steps.

1. *Identify the individual accounts involved in the transaction or event.*

2. *Classify the accounts in step 1 as Assets, Liabilities, or Owners' Equity.*

3. *Determine whether the accounts are increasing or decreasing. (Remember that Revenues will be a credit because they increase Owners' Equity, and expenses will be a debit because expenses decrease Owners' Equity.)*

4. *Record the transaction according to the "crutch."* **(See Exhibit 2.2)**

EXHIBIT 2.2

CRUTCH					
Assets		**Liabilities**		**Owners' Equity**	
Debit (Left)	Credit (Right)	Debit (Left)	Credit (Right)	Debit (Left)	Credit (Right)
Increase	Decrease	Decrease	Increase	Decrease	Increase
+	–	–	+	–	+
				Expenses	Revenues

Returning to the previous example, where the firm borrowed $50 cash, the steps are:

1. *The accounts are Cash and Note Payable.*

2. *Cash is an Asset; Note Payable is a Liability.*

3. *Cash is increasing; Note Payable is increasing.*

4. *Cash increases on the left (debit) and Note Payable increases on the right (credit).*

Therefore:

Debit	Credit	Debit $	Credit $
Cash		50	
	Note Payable		50

This is so much fun, let's do another one. Let's sell inventory that costs $100 for $220 cash.

1. *The accounts involved in the transaction are Cash, Inventory, Sales, and Cost of Goods Sold.*

2. *Cash is an Asset; Inventory is an Asset; Sales and Cost of Goods Sold affect Owners' Equity.*

3. *Cash is increasing; Inventory is decreasing; Sales increase Owners' Equity; Cost of Goods Sold decreases Owners' Equity.*

4. *Referring to the crutch, Cash increases on the left; Inventory decreases on the right; Owners' Equity increases on the right (from the Sale) and decreases on the left (from the Cost of Goods Sold).*

Therefore:

Debit	Credit	Debit $	Credit $
Cash		220	
	Sales		220
Cost of Goods Sold		100	
	Inventory		100

Below, we repeat the example from the previous chapter, using both intuitive and conventional formats.

The accounting events and journal entries are as follows.

1. Borrow $100 cash.

Assets	Liabilities	Owners' Equity
100 Cash	100 Note Payable	

Cash		100	
	Note Payable		100

2. Sell stock to investors for $100 cash.

Assets	Liabilities	Owners' Equity
100 Cash		100 Stock

Cash		100	
	Stock		100

3. Buy a building for $80 cash.

Assets	Liabilities	Owners' Equity
80 Building (80) Cash		

Building		80	
	Cash		80

4. Buy inventory for $40 cash

Assets	Liabilities	Owners' Equity
40 Inventory (40) Cash		

Inventory		40	
	Cash		40

5. Sell half of the inventory for $80 cash.

Assets	Liabilities	Owners' Equity
80 Cash (20) Inventory		80 Revenue (20) COGS

Cash		80	
	Revenue		80
COGS		20	
	Inventory		20

6. Pay wages of $10 cash.

Assets	Liabilities	Owners' Equity
(10) Cash		(10) Wage Expense

Wage Expense		10	
	Cash		10

7. Depreciate the building by $20.

Assets	Liabilities	Owners' Equity
(20) Building (or A/D)		(20) Depreciation Expense

Depreciation Expense		20	
	Building (or A/D)		20

8. Book $10 of interest expense to be paid later.

Assets	Liabilities	Owners' Equity
	10 Interest Payable	(10) Interest Expense

Interest Expense		10	
	Interest Payable		10

9. Book $7 of tax expense to be paid later.

Assets	Liabilities	Owners' Equity
	7 Tax Payable	(7) Tax Expense

Tax Expense		7	
	Tax Payable		7

10. The firm closes all temporary accounts.

Assets	Liabilities	Owners' Equity
		(80) Revenue 20 Cost of Goods Sold 10 Wage Expense 20 Depreciation Expense 10 Interest Expense 7 Tax Expense 13 Retained Earnings

Revenue		80	
	Cost of Goods Sold		20
	Wage Expense		10
	Depreciation Expense		20
	Interest Expense		10
	Tax Expense		7
	Retained Earnings		13

The closing entry in conventional format has a debit to Revenue and a credit to all expenses. This reverses the original entries in order to set the revenue and expense balances to zero, as seen in the ledger. **(See Exhibit 2.3)**

EXHIBIT 2.3

Event	Assets	Cash	Inventory	Building	Total	Liabilities	Note Payable	Interest Payable	Taxes Payable	Total Liabilities	Owners' Equity	Stock	Retained Earnings	Total Owners' Equity	Total Liabilities & Owners' Equity	Revenue	Cost of Goods Sold	Wage Expense	Depreciation Expense	Interest Expense	Tax Expense
Begin	0	0	0	0	0	0	0	0	0	0	0	0	0	0							
1		100					100														
2		100										100									
3		(80)		80																	
4		(40)	40																		
5		80														80					
5		(20)															(20)				
6		(10)																(10)			
7			(20)																(20)		
8								10												(10)	
9									7												(7)
10													13			(80)	20	10	20	10	7
End		150	20	60	230		100	10	7	117		100	13	113	230	0	0	0	0	0	0

Aside from journal entries, there is one more aspect to the difference between intuitive and conventional formats, and it pertains to the form of the ledger.

Thus far, we have shown the ledger as a table (as per above), representing an equation, with opening balances, changes in account balances, and ending balances in adjacent rows. Some texts will show the ledger in T-account format. When we look at the "crutch" **(Exhibit 2.2)** we observe that the left and the right sides of each section of the Balance Sheet form a ◀**"T"**▶. This "T" is the conventional way of tracking account balances in the ledger. The conventional format (as a "T-account") is shown below for the inventory account only.

Inventory	
Beginning Balance	
Increases	Decreases
Ending Balance	

Inventory	
Beginning Balance	
Purchases	Cost of Goods Sold
Ending Balance	

Inventory	
0	
40	20
20	

We will use the equation form of the ledger in this text, rather than the "T-account" form.

We now turn to some foundational, theoretical issues. These will help us gain a better understanding of accounting issues and will help us analyze the financial statements of firms in fairly sophisticated ways.

LIFE CYCLE OF THE FIRM AND THE "NET INCOME/CASH FLOW PROFILE"

The life cycle of a firm consists of the following four phases: introduction (intro), growth, maturity, and decline. It is instructive to look at a graph of a time series of a firm's cash flows and Net Income to identify where the firm might be in its life cycle. Knowing where the firm is in its life cycle helps us understand its capital needs (the relative use of outside financing and internally generated capital) and helps us make predictions about its future. Below is a generic version of such a graph. Explanations follow. **(See Exhibit 3.1)**

EXHIBIT 3.1

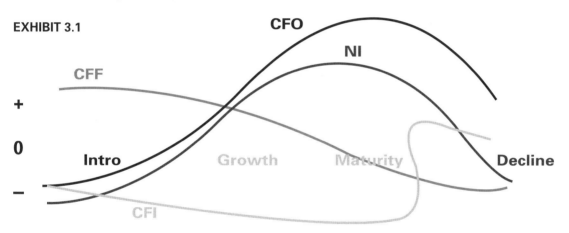

When firms are just getting started, they usually have negative Net Income (NI) and negative Cash from Operations (CFO). This happens because it takes time (and money) to "set up shop," identify a customer base, market to the customers, buy and deliver inventory, etc.

Additionally, the firm is investing in infrastructure (equipment and buildings, e.g.), so its Cash for Investing (CFI) will be negative. This means that cash is "going out" of the firm into these long-lived assets.

If Net Income, operating cash flows and investing cash flows are all negative, the firm will definitely need outside sources of cash. Without cash, nothing happens. Thus, Cash from Financing (CFF) will be positive. Cash will come from lenders and investors.

During the "growth phase," operating cash flows cease being as negative and eventually turn positive. We say that the firm becomes "cash flow positive," meaning that operating cash flows become positive. Investing cash flows will likely remain negative as the firm continues to spend cash on various long-lived assets such as buildings and equipment. Financing cash flows often continue positive during the growth phase, since the firm still needs outside financing in order to fund its growing operations and investments in buildings, etc.

During the "mature" phase, operating cash flows are generally positive. Investing cash flows slow down as the firm has fewer investment opportunities. For instance, if the firm is in the retail sector, it may have saturated so many markets already that there are no "street corners" left on which to put a new store. Also in the mature phase, financing cash flows often turn negative, as the firm starts to pay down debt and to return cash to investors in the form of share repurchases and dividends.

Finally, during the decline phase, the firm's operating cash flows can turn negative as the firm is unable to sustain healthy operations. We see this happening in some technology sectors as the firm may not have switched to new technologies quickly enough. Examples would include typewriter and print film manufacturers. If operating cash flows turn negative, the firm may try to seek outside financing through new loans or stock issues. However, often these are difficult to obtain in a distressed environment and therefore financing cash flows do not turn back positive, even though the firm may need the outside funding. In extreme circumstances, the government steps in and provides public capital, although history suggests that this may not be wise (for taxpayers). Firms may have to resort to selling assets to raise cash. In this case, investing cash flows can become positive. Positive investing cash flow means that the firm is liquidating assets to raise cash.

THE MAIN GOAL: PREDICTION OF FUTURE CASH FLOWS

Lenders and investors primarily read financial reports to help them make predictions about firms' futures.

Ultimately, the prediction that matters most is the prediction of cash flow.

- *Will the firm be able to generate enough cash to run the daily operations of the business?*

- *Will it have enough cash left over to make investments in order to maintain its current asset base and invest in new assets for the future?*

- *Will it have enough cash to satisfy the demands of lenders and investors?*

Research analysts use information from the financial reports, as well as guidance from conference calls and press releases, to make predictions of future Financial Statements. Future Financial Statements are called ◀**pro forma statements,**▶ or forecasted statements. One of the primary purposes of pro forma statements is to try to determine the firm's future cash flows. Most decisions concerning firms (for example, whether to buy a firm's stock or to lend money to a firm) require an estimate of the firm's future cash flows and sustainable cash generating ability.

AN INTRODUCTION TO THE FINANCING DILEMMA: DEBT VS. EQUITY

We have mentioned the two main sources of outside financing: lenders and investors. Equity financing (that is, cash from investors) is sometimes called "soft" financing, since the firm does not have to pay back the money received from investors. That is, the firm is usually not obligated to buy back the stock. If equity holders want "out," they can simply sell their stock to other investors, assuming the stock is traded on a stock exchange. Firms do not even have to pay dividends to stockholders. Dividends are optional.

Conversely, debt must be repaid. Interest must also be paid on the borrowed money. Thus, debt financing is sometimes called "hard financing," because of this requirement to pay interest and to pay back principal.

However, debt financing is often advantageous. It is usually cheaper than equity financing since debt is usually (but not always) less risky. It is less risky to the extent that debtholders can use various legal means to protect their claims, such as requiring collateral or limiting the use of the borrowed money. When risk is lower, the lender will charge a lower interest rate.

By contrast, stockholders do not have the same ability to protect their claims through collateral. Since stockholders assume more risk, they demand a higher return on their investment.

- -
A WORD ON TERMINOLOGY

"Stockholders" is another way of describing the owners of equity. That is, the equity owner has purchased the firm's stock (shares of ownership in the firm).
- -

The relationship between risk of an investment and expected return on the investment is from a famous theory from finance, but it also makes intuitive sense. When risk is lower, the return that outside sources of financing will require is reduced.

Debt is cheaper for another reason. Governments often subsidize debt financing by allowing tax deductions for interest payments. On the other hand, dividends are usually not deductible. Deductions reduce the amount of taxable income and therefore the amount of money that firms would have to pay the government for taxes.

Therefore, debt has a tax advantage that makes it relatively cheaper than equity.

The use of debt has another advantage. It allows the firm to ◀leverage▶ earnings to the benefit of shareholders. Debtholders' claims on the assets of the firm are limited to the debt agreement. That is, debtholders can expect to receive the interest and the return of principal (at maturity, that is, when the debt must be repaid). If the firm is able to borrow at, say 6%, and then generate returns of, say 20%, by putting the borrowed money to work, the extra earnings will accrue to the shareholders. Debtholders do not participate in the extra returns. They get only their fixed interest (6%) plus principal.

ASK THE ACCOUNTING GURU

A mix between debt and equity is called a "convertible" or "convertible debt". The terms of these hybrid investment vehicles vary but typically take the form of debt that are convertible into shares of stock. In other words, the debtholders earn a fixed return, but they could convert to stockholders and share in the extra returns. Perhaps the best of both worlds? Maybe. Once the conversion to shares of stock has been made, the investor has lost this debtholder status and is now an equityholder. It takes a very sophisticated lender/investor to successfully capture the extra returns associated with convertibles.

The above illustrates another dimension to the financing dilemma, namely the conflict that arises between debtholders and stockholders. Debtholders do not want management to take much risk. They want management to "play it safe" so that they will have sufficient cash to pay interest and to pay back the principal.

Stockholders, on the other hand, are generally risk-takers. They want management to invest in riskier projects that they nonetheless expect to be winners. We call these projects "positive net present value" (NPV) projects. A short way of describing a positive NPV investment is simply to say that the expected benefits from the investment exceed the cost of the investment.

A numerical example will illustrate the leveraging effect of debt.

Suppose a firm borrows $10, issues stock for $10, and buys inventory with the entire $20. Then, the firm sells the inventory for $30 cash. That is, the firm is able to sell the inventory at a 50% markup above cost. ($30 = 20 + 50% * 20). The bank charges a 10% interest rate. Then suppose that the firm pays back all of the borrowed money, as well as $1 for interest ($1=10% interest rate *$10).

Let's journalize the events below.

1. The issue of debt would be journalized as follows:

Assets	Liabilities	Owners' Equity
10 Cash	10 Debt	

2. The issue of stock is booked as follows:

Assets	Liabilities	Owners' Equity
10 Cash		10 Stock

3. The purchase of the inventory is journalized as follows:

Assets	Liabilities	Owners' Equity
(20) Cash		
20 Inventory		

4. The sale of the inventory is shown below:

Assets	Liabilities	Owners' Equity
30 Cash		30 Revenue
(20) Inventory		(20) Cost of Goods Sold

5. The debtholders will be paid their interest ($1) and principal ($10), as shown below in events 5 and 6:

Assets	Liabilities	Owners' Equity
(1) Cash		(1) Interest Expense

6.

Assets	Liabilities	Owners' Equity
(10) Cash	(10) Debt	

Now, let us take a picture of where we are. We will do so by posting the above events to the ledger and creating the Balance Sheet. (For simplicity, we will post Revenues, Cost of Goods Sold, and Interest Expense directly in Retained Earnings and will not do the closing entry.)

		Cash	Inventory	Debt	Stock	Retained Earnings
	Begin	0	0	0	0	0
Event Numbers	1	10		10		
	2	10			10	
	3	(20)	20			
	4	30				30
	4		(20)			(20)
	5	(1)				(1)
	6	(10)		(10)		
	End	19	0	0	10	9

One way to measure the returns to the debtholders and stockholders is to calculate the earnings generated by the respective investments in the firm (the loan of $10 and the stock investment of $10).

The debtholders received $1 per $10 of loan, meaning that they got a return of 10%, or exactly equal to the required interest rate ($1 / $10 = 10%).

On the other hand, stockholders earned $9 ($10 of profit on the sale of the inventory, less $1 for interest on the debt) per $10 of stock invested in the firm, or 90% ($9 / $10 = 90%)).

If the firm had not borrowed the money, it would have had only $10 of cash, rather than $20, and it would have therefore bought only $10 of inventory. Assuming the same 50% markup above cost, the firm would have sold the inventory for $15 (15 = 10 + 50%*10). Net Income would have been $5 ($15 Revenue – 10 Cost of Goods Sold). Thus, the return to the shareholders would have been 50% ($5 of profit on the sale of inventory / $10 of stock invested), compared to 90%.

The important point is that the firm uses borrowed money that "costs" 10% and generates returns that are greater than the cost of the borrowing. The extra returns accrue to the stockholders, not to the debtholders, because debtholders' claims are fixed (10% for the interest).

Debt financing clearly has advantages, even though it must be paid back. However, there can be "too much of a good thing" when it comes to debt. Debt can be a double-edged sword. As in the initial case previously, suppose that the firm borrows $10, sells stock for $10, and buys $20 of inventory. However, now assume that the firm sells the inventory for only $15, rather than $30, resulting in a net loss on the sale of $5 (15 – 20). These events are journalized below.

1. The issue of debt is below:

Assets	Liabilities	Owners' Equity
10 Cash	10 Debt	

2. The issue of stock is booked as follows:

Assets	Liabilities	Owners' Equity
10 Cash		10 Stock

3. The purchase of the inventory is journalized as follows:

Assets	Liabilities	Owners' Equity
(20) Cash		
20 Inventory		

4. All inventory is sold for $15 cash:

Assets	Liabilities	Owners' Equity
15 Cash		15 Revenue
(20) Inventory		(20) Cost of Goods Sold

5. The debtholders would still demand their interest and principal, as before and repeated below:

Assets	Liabilities	Owners' Equity
(1) Cash		(1) Interest Expense

6.

Assets	Liabilities	Owners' Equity
(10) Cash	(10) Debt	

The firm would have the below ledger and Balance Sheet.

		Cash	Inventory	Debt	Stock	Retained Earnings
	Begin	0	0	0	0	0
Event Numbers	1	10		10		
	2	10			10	
	3	(20)	20			
	4	15				15
	4		(20)			(20)
	5	(1)				(1)
	6	(10)		(10)		
	End	4	0	0	10	(6)

In this case, the return to shareholders is negative 60% (-6/10), but the return to debtholders is still 10%. Debtholders neither share in the excess positive returns nor in the negative returns. Their returns are fixed. The excess positive returns and the negative returns accrue to stockholders. The important point for now is that the choice of outside financing has clear and major implications for the firm. Thus, once a firm has cash, it is fungible, meaning that it is interchangeable. We say "cash is cash is cash is cash." However, the source of cash matters. Cash comes into the firm with different obligations and responsibilities attached to it.

A BIT OF PERSPECTIVE

Advising firms how to capitalize.(debt versus equity) is also known as the practice of Corporate Finance, an important source of advisory income to an Investment Bank.

Another way that the effects of leverage can be viewed is provided in **Exhibit 3.2**, where we show a firm with $1,000 in sales in "Case 1." The ◀**Variable Operating Expenses▶** are all the expenses that are necessary to generate sales and that vary with sales. Examples are Cost of Goods Sold and many of the Selling, General, and Administrative (SG&A) Expenses. In Case 1, these are assumed to be $600.

The subtotal, **◄Earnings before Interest and Taxes►** (often abbreviated EBIT), is therefore $400. Assume that the firm has debt that incurs Interest Expense of $200. Interest Expense is considered a "fixed" expense since it does not vary with revenue. Rather, Interest Expense varies with the amount of debt and the interest rate charged on the debt. We assume a tax rate of 40%, leaving the firm with Net Income of $120.

In Case 2 of **Exhibit 3.2**, assume that revenue increases by 10%, from $1,000 to $1,100. Variable Operating Expenses will also increase by 10% by definition, and EBIT increases by 10% (from $400 to $440). Interest does not vary with revenue, however. The effect of fixed expenses magnifies the effect on Net Income, which increases by 20%, from $120 to $144. The magnification of the 10% increase on revenue to a 20% increase on Net Income is called **◄financial leverage►** and results from the fixed Interest Expense.

However, again notice the "double-edged sword." When revenue falls by 10% (in Case 3 of **Exhibit 3.2**), Net Income falls by 20%, since the interest is still incurred at the same level of $200.

We now turn to another part of the big picture—institutional settings.

INSTITUTIONAL AND THEORETICAL BACKGROUND

The SEC

The SEC is authorized by U.S. law to write U.S. GAAP. However, the SEC has relied on the expertise in the private sector, in particular the FASB. The FASB is an independent rule-making body that is funded through fees paid by publicly traded firms.

The SEC's authority was granted by the U.S. Congress. The stock market "crash" of 1929 prompted the U.S. Congress (in 1933 and 1934) to institute changes that would hopefully reduce the likelihood of a repeat crash. Congress passed the Securities Act in 1933 and the Securities Exchange Act in 1934. The Securities Act of 1933 regulates IPOs of securities—both stocks and bonds. The 1934 Securities Exchange Act regulates the subsequent trading of securities. It also created the SEC—the police that enforces the 1933 Act.

Overall, the purpose of the SEC is to ensure that full and fair disclosures are made to all investors before initial offerings and then afterwards in the secondary markets.

To register securities for initial sale, firms file a registration statement. The main part of the registration statement is the prospectus, which includes:

* *audited Financial Statements*
* *a description of the intended use of the money raised through the public offering*
* *a description of the risks of the securities*
* *a description of the lines of business in which the firm operates*

EXHIBIT 3.2

	Case 1	Case 2	% change from Case 1 to Case 2	Case 3	% change from Case 1 to Case 3
Revenue	1,000	1,100	10%	900	(10%)
Variable Operating Expenses	(600)	(660)	10%	(540)	(10%)
Earnings before Interest and Taxes (EBIT)	400	440	10%	360	(10%)
Interest on Fixed Rate Debt	(200)	(200)	0%	(200)	(0%)
Pre-tax Income	200	240	20%	160	(20%)
Taxes (40%)	(80)	(96)		(64)	
Net Income	120	144	20%	96	(20%)

The SEC has been urging firms to provide registration statements written in "plain English" so that vital information is clearly understood by every potential buyer of the securities. A plain English manual is even available on the SEC's website.

Major subsequent filings (after the registration statement) include:

- ◀**Form 10-K**▶ *(annual filing, which includes the basic Financial Statements and notes plus other non-financial information)*

- ◀**Form 10-Q**▶ *(quarterly filing of financial and non-financial information)*

- ◀**Form 8-K**▶ *(filing after a significant event occurs, such as changes in directors, officers, or accountants)*

- ◀**Proxy**▶ *(request for voting rights to be exercised at the annual shareholders' meetings) Shareholders have the right to vote for directors of the firm and on other important matters, which are described in the proxy. Also included in the proxy is information on executive compensation.*

A WORD ON TERMINOLOGY

10-Ks are required filings for all publicly traded firms in the U.S. Firms may also elect to prepare another report called an Annual Report which is not required by the SEC. Annual Reports can be found in the "Investor Relations" section of a firm's website. The difference between an Annual Report and a 10-K is sometimes negligible. However, Annual Reports are often prepared for a wider array of users such as customers, potential employees and the main stream press and are, therefore, more marketing oriented often with color photographs and charts depicting the firm's business and performance. Well prepared users of a firm's information will often read both the Annual Report and the 10-K.

HINT

The technical form number assigned by the SEC to Proxies are Definitive 14-As or "Def 14-A" for short. Other important information that you can find in Proxies include who the firm considers to be its peers (or firms with operations comparable to their operations). This type of insight is extremely helpful when analyzing a firm.

The SEC has begun the transition to electronic filing. Firms will be required to file their 10-Ks and other forms electronically, using the taxonomy of eXtensible-Business-Reporting Language, or XBRL. XBRL will expedite and standardize the filing of firms' Financial Statements. This will allow lenders and investors to have faster access to the information and to be able to compare financial information of one firm to other firms because the data will be standardized.

Now let's address a question of "why." Why do we need monitors, such as the SEC, over the Financial Accounting process?

AGENCY THEORY: THE NEED FOR CONTRACTS AND REGULATORY OVERSIGHT

The reason for the SEC, as well as for other institutions charged with protecting participants in capital markets, stems from the agency problem. The agency problem arises whenever one party (the principal) delegates work to another party (the agent). The principal wants the agent to act on the principal's behalf, but the agent may desire to fulfill his or her own goals that will not coincide with those of the principal.

> Other regulators around the world charged with protecting capital markets include the Financial Services Authority (FSA) in the U.K., the Securities and Futures Commission (SFC) in Hong Kong, and the Australian Securities & Investment Commission (ASIC). The worldwide list is too large to convey in this text as nearly every country or province within a country has formed regulatory bodies to manage these challenges and protect participants in capital markets.

In the context of firms, owners are the principals, who hire professional managers, who are the agents, to run the firm. Owners will want managers to take certain actions that increase firm value, but managers may desire to maximize their own pay, including perquisites. Thus, the goals of the principal and those of the agent will not coincide.

One solution to the agency problem is effective hiring, namely hiring managers who are capable, will work hard, and will work in the interest of the owners. Of course, owners (principals) cannot be sure that they will find and hire the right people (agents).

For example, will the agent have the ability to perform the assigned duties? The principal cannot determine with certainty, before the fact, an agent's "type." Unknown type is referred to as the problem of "adverse selection." That is, the principal may hire a dud, or someone who will work against the goals of the principal.

Besides the problem of adverse selection, another issue pertains to an agent's effort. Namely, will the agent not only possess the ability but also put forth the right amount of effort on behalf of the principal? The agent may be lazy, or the agent's effort may be directed toward self enrichment at the expense of the principal. Unknown effort is referred to as the problem of "moral hazard." There is a hazard (a moral hazard) that the hired agent will work at cross-purposes to the principal.

Cures for the problems of adverse selection and moral hazard include monitoring and incentive contracting.

Owners could directly monitor the actions of managers after they are hired, but this is costly for them to do personally. Instead, they hire monitors, and they rely on monitors that are mandated by law. Included in the group of monitors are: the SEC, the external auditor, the internal auditor, the legal profession, the media, "industry watchdogs," and boards of directors. Each of these has a cost, but the benefits are presumed to outweigh the costs. Further, there is an implicit cost sharing among all beneficiaries of society. For example, the SEC is publicly funded. Therefore, all taxpayers pay for the SEC's oversight, even though not every taxpayer may participate as a lender or investor.

Another cure for the agency problem is sharing some of the risk and rewards of the outcomes with the agent. This solution is referred to as incentive contracting. The theory is that agents will act in a manner that is consistent with the incentives provided in their compensation packages. For instance, if an owner wants an agent to increase, say, a firm's earnings, then the owner can reward the agent with a bonus that is dependent upon earnings. If the owner wants the stock price to rise, then the principal (owner) could include stock or stock options in the agent's (manager's) pay package. Additionally, equity compensation (stock and stock options) turns the manager into an owner, which further aligns the goals of the principal with the agent.

To complicate matters, however, especially within the corporate framework, managers, in exercising their responsibilities to owners, must often balance the desires of other constituencies with those of the owners. This seems contradictory. After all, if managers are responsible only to owners, why worry about anyone else?

This question is not just rhetorical but is the basis of an active debate in the law and in larger society. Are firms responsible to their communities, to their workers, for the environment, or are they focused on satisfying only one provider of capital—equity holders?

To ensure that managers do not exploit other constituencies, legal protections have been developed. For instance, assume a bank loans money to a firm. What are the responsibilities of managers to creditors? Can the managers of the firm who got the money pay themselves more and give all the rest to shareholders as a dividend? Managers would be better off, as well as shareholders, so what does agency theory offer in this type of situation?

These questions illustrate that agency problems are not one dimensional, but rather that firms operate within a multi-dimensional agency environment. Managers are answerable to creditors and if they exploit creditors, their firm's ◀credit rating▶ will fall, increasing the cost of borrowing money in the future, thereby potentially hurting the growth potential of the firm, and thus the firm's owners. Further, just to be sure that they are protected, creditors will place restrictions on managers through certain provisions in their loans. For instance, creditors may place restrictions on what the firm may do with the borrowed money. Aware of this "agency cost of debt" (the increased cost of borrowing from exploitation of creditors, along with restrictive covenants), managers find that they must balance the interests of the debtholders with the interest of equity holders. This complicated agency environment extends to other constituencies, leading some to consider the corporation to be a "nexus" of relationships and contracts.

> Some of the more well known credit rating services in the world are Moodys, Standard & Poor's, Fitch and A.M. Best. These rating services are paid to analyze the riskiness of a firm's debt.

ACCOUNTING PRINCIPLES

Accounting rules can be written on an ad hoc basis or can be based upon an underlying theory. The FASB and the IASB have tried to do the latter by conforming to a coherent set of principles, assumptions, and constraints. The following provides an overview of some theoretical issues and some additional vocabulary.

The principles established by the accounting profession include the Revenue Principle, the Expense (or matching) Principle, the Cost Principle, and the Full Disclosure Principle.

The Revenue and Matching Principles: the Basis of Accrual Accounting

Firms often book revenues even though no cash is received at the time of the sale. Similarly, firms often book expenses even though no cash is paid at the time that the expense is recognized. In these instances, firms create an Account Receivable or Account Payable for the revenue and expense, respectively.

On the flip side, it is also possible that firms do not book revenues upon receipt of cash from a customer, nor book an expense upon payment of cash to a supplier. The reasons for revenues and expenses not corresponding to cash receipts and cash disbursements pertain to accrual accounting. ◀Accrual accounting▶ is based upon two principles: the Revenue Principle and the Matching Principle.

◀The Revenue Principle▶ says to book (record, recognize, journalize) revenue when it is earned and it is realized or realizable. Realizable means that the receivable will **likely** turn into cash. Therefore, the Revenue Principle says that non-cash sales can be called sales (that is, officially booked as sales) if the receivable is *realizable* (likely to turn into cash). The Revenue Principle also says that firms will **not** have a sale, even if the customer has paid cash to the firm, *if* the firm has not *earned* the revenue.

For instance, a consulting firm may receive an up-front payment from a client for a consulting project. The firm records the cash increase, but the firm does not yet have revenue because it has not yet performed the service (i.e., the firm has not earned it). As another example, consider a retailer who sells a gift card. The retailer may receive cash payment for the gift card, but it may not book revenue until the card is redeemed (used) by the holder of the gift card.

◀**The Expense Principle (also called the "Matching Principle")▶** says to book the expense when the benefit is received regardless of the timing of the cash flow. The expense is to be matched with the revenue (the benefit), hence the name Matching Principle.

Therefore, the booking of revenue or expense does not necessarily correspond to cash flows. The cash flow may occur either before or after the booking of the revenue or expense. Below, we describe the various variations of revenues and expenses.

> These are key concepts! The receipt of cash does not trigger revenue and the disbursement of cash does not trigger an expense.

Revenues

(See the journal entries below. All amounts are assumed to be $100 for illustration purposes.)

1. Is a cash sale.

2a. Is a credit sale (earned but not realized).

2b. Is the receipt of cash from the credit sale in 2a.

3a. Is unearned revenue (realized but not earned). Unearned revenues are liabilities.

3b. Is recognition of revenue after shipping the product or performing the service.

1. Cash sale

Assets	Liabilities	Owners' Equity
100 Cash		100 Revenue

2a. Credit sale (also called an accrued sale)

Assets	Liabilities	Owners' Equity
100 A/R		100 Revenue

2b. Cash collection of the above credit sale

Assets	Liabilities	Owners' Equity
100 Cash (100) A/R		

3a. Unearned revenue (also called Deferred Revenue or Advances from Customers)

Assets	Liabilities	Owners' Equity
100 Cash	100 Unearned Revenue	

3b. Earned revenue that had been previously booked as unearned

Assets	Liabilities	Owners' Equity
	(100) Unearned Revenue	100 Revenue

3a and 3b correspond to the gift card example described earlier. 3a would be the sale of the gift card by the retailer. 3b would be the redemption of the gift card by the card holder, at which point the retailer has earned the revenue.

Expenses

4. Is a cash expense.

5a. Is an accrued expense (benefit has been received but not paid for).

5b. Is the payment of the accrued expense in 5a.

6a. Is a deferred or prepaid expense (paid for) but the benefit has not been received. Prepaid expenses are assets.

6b. Is an expense that reflects the use of the asset that was booked in 6a.

4. Cash expense

Assets	Liabilities	Owners' Equity
(100) Cash		(100) Expense

5a. Accrued expense

Assets	Liabilities	Owners' Equity
	100 Payable	(100) Expense

5b. Cash payment of accrued expense

Assets	Liabilities	Owners' Equity
(100) Cash	(100) Payable	

5a and 5b are quite common. Wages Payable, Utilities Payable, Taxes Payable, and Interest Payable, among others are common types of expenses that are paid for after the firm has received and recognized the service or benefit. Firms typically prefer to defer the cash payments for these and other services, to the extent possible, since it helps with their liquidity needs.

6a. Prepaid Expense (also called Deferred Expense)

Assets	Liabilities	Owners' Equity
100 Prepaid Expense (100) Cash		

6b. Expensing Prepaid Expenses

Assets	Liabilities	Owners' Equity
(100) Prepaid Expense		(100) Cash

In contrast to 5a and 5b, 6a and 6b are situations where a firm must pay for a service or benefit in advance. Typically, firms must prepay rent and insurance. At the beginning of a rental period, payment is due. Similarly, at the beginning of a period over which the firm receives insurance protection, the insurance premium is due. At the end of the respective periods, the firm would adjust the Prepaid Expense account and recognize a prorated amount of Rent Expense or Insurance Expense.

example

One common situation a firm will encounter is when it makes mid-year payments for multi-year contracts. Assume on April 1, Year "X," a firm prepays rent for 2 years. The amount of the prepayment is $12,000, or $6,000 per year. Below we record the transactions on the payment date and on each subsequent date shown below.

April 1, X

Assets	Liabilities	Owners' Equity
(12,000) Cash 12,000 Prepaid Rent		

December 31, X, Fiscal Year End (FYE)

Assets	Liabilities	Owners' Equity
(4,500) Prepaid Rent		(4,500) Rent Expense

4,500 = 9/12 * 6,000. The period from April through December contains nine months. Since the firm occupied the property for 9/12 of the year, it will expense 9/12 of one year's worth of Prepaid Rent.

December 31, Y (FYE)

Assets	Liabilities	Owners' Equity
(6,000) Prepaid Rent		(6,000) Rent Expense

6,000 = 12/12 * 6,000. On December 31, Y, the firm will recognize one full year of Rent Expense and reduce the Prepaid Rent accordingly.

March 31, Z

Assets	Liabilities	Owners' Equity
(1,500) Prepaid Rent		(1,500) Rent Expense

The firm recognizes $1,500 (3/12 * 6,000) in Year Z because there are three remaining months on the two-year rental agreement.

The Cost Principle

‹**The Cost Principle**› pertains mainly to the measurement of asset purchases. Assets are recorded on the Balance Sheet at their cost, which means their cash value, or cash equivalent value. (Cash equivalent means the present value of future cash flows. We will discuss present value briefly in an upcoming chapter.) The Cost Principle requires inclusion of all cash or cash equivalent outlays to bring the asset to its place of intended use by the firm. Thus, the cost of a machine would include not only the invoice price, but also shipping, insurance, and installation.

example

A firm buys a machine with an invoice price of $1,000. The firm must also pay shipping of $50 and insurance while in transit of $30. Installation of the machine is $300. Under the Cost Principle, the machine would be booked at a total value of $1,380 (1,000 + 50 + 30 + 300). Assuming cash was paid for all of the charges, the journal entry would be as follows:

Assets	Liabilities	Owners' Equity
1,380 Equipment (1,380) Cash		

A WORD ON TERMINOLOGY

The Cost Principle is often referred to as "historical cost".

The Full Disclosure Principle

The Full Disclosure Principle pertains both to what is disclosed and how it is disclosed. Firms must disclose all "relevant" financial information. Relevant information is all information that would make a difference in the decisions of a "reasonable" lender or investor. Another manifestation of the Full Disclosure Principle is the classified presentation of the Financial Statements.

For example, the Balance Sheet has the following categories:

- *Current Assets*
- *Noncurrent Assets*
- *Current Liabilities*
- *Noncurrent Liabilities*
- *Owners' Equity*

◀**Current assets**▶ are cash, items that will convert to cash (such as Accounts Receivable), or that will be used or consumed (such as Inventory and Prepaid Insurance) within one year. Noncurrent Assets are simply assets which are not classified as Current.

◀**Current liabilities**▶ will be liquidated within one year. Noncurrent Liabilities are simply not Current Liabilities. Owners' Equity is the algebraic remains (Assets – Liabilities). It constitutes the claims of the owners.

Under U.S. GAAP, assets are listed in the Balance Sheet in the order of ◀**liquidity**▶ ("nearness" to cash or use). Thus, typically the order will be:

- *Cash*
- *Accounts Receivable*
- *Marketable Investments (investments in the stock and bonds of other companies)*
- *Inventory*
- *Prepaid Rent and Insurance*
- *Property Plant and Equipment*
- *Intangible Assets (Patents, Goodwill, etc.)*

Liabilities are listed in the order of ◀**maturity**▶, that is, when they have to be paid. Typically, the order will be as follows:

- *Accounts Payable*
- *Wages Payable*
- *Taxes Payable*
- *Short Term Debt*
- *Long Term Debt*
- *Bonds Payable (a type of Debt)*

Owners' Equity is listed in the order of permanence. By permanence, we mean the degree to which the firm would pay owners a return on their ◀**investments**▶ (dividends) or buy back the stock (share repurchases). Firms are not required to pay dividends or repurchase shares, but it is not unusual for them to do so. The most permanent Owners' Equity account is the Stock account. Retained Earnings is considered less permanent because dividends are paid from (reduce) Retained Earnings. Therefore, the order of presentation will be as follows. (We will add more Owners' Equity accounts in a later chapter.)

- *Stock*
- *Retained Earnings*

The Income Statement is categorized in the following way:

- *Operating Section, which includes Sales (Revenues); Cost of Goods Sold (COGS); Selling, General, and Administrative Expense (SG&A Expense); Research and Development Expense (R&D Expense); and Depreciation Expense.*

- *Non-operating Section, which includes Interest Expense and Investment Income (income earned on investments in the stocks and bonds of other firms)*

- *Income Tax Expense (also called, "Provision for Income Taxes")*

- *Discontinued Operations (often called "Disc Ops" for short, which are entire segments of the firm's operations that it plans to sell)*

- *Extraordinary Items (various gains and losses that are unusual and infrequent)*

MORE TERMINOLOGY FOR THE INCOME STATEMENT

Users of Financial Statements often refer to "The Line" when analyzing a firm.

- **"Above the Line"** refers to the results from a firm's central, ongoing operations.

- **"Below the Line"** refers to all of the firm's other results (Non-operating, Income Taxes, Discontinued Operations and Extraordinary Items).

The classified Income Statement is structured to help investors assess earnings quality. The Operating Section contains the earnings from central, ongoing operations, and it is often referred to as EBIT. EBIT is considered a high quality component of Net Income because it is deemed to be more sustainable.

As we have seen in the opening chapter, the Statement of Cash Flows must be classified in the following way:

- *Cash From Operating Activities*
- *Cash From Investing Activities*
- *Cash From Financing Activities*

Another manifestation of the Full Disclosure Principle is the use of ◀**contra accounts**▶. These are accounts that are used to re-value other accounts. We saw an example of a contra-account in Accumulated Depreciation. Rather than reducing the Property, Plant, and Equipment (PP&E) account directly (for depreciation) we reduce it indirectly by setting up the Accumulated Depreciation account. In this way, we know the original cost of the PP&E and we know how much of it has been depreciated. Firms use contra-accounts for other asset accounts, as well as for some liability, owners' equity, and revenue accounts. We will see examples of other contra-accounts later.

USERS, QUALITATIVE CHARACTERISTICS, AND THE CONSERVATISM CONSTRAINT

Users: The intended users of financial reports are any interested parties with a reasonable understanding of business and with a willingness to study the reports with reasonable diligence. The interested parties include investors, lenders, labor unions, the government, and competitors.

Qualitative Characteristics: The disclosures made in the financial reports should be relevant and reliable. Relevant means that the information can affect decisions. It also means that the information should be timely. If the disclosures are too old, they are "history," and thus irrelevant. To be reliable, the information must be neutral (not systematically biased up or down) and verifiable. These two attributes of relevance and reliability are often in tension. For example, current fair values of buildings may be relevant for an investor or for a loan officer at a bank. However, fair values of buildings may not be very reliable because they often must be estimated by appraisers who would have differing opinions. On the other hand, historical cost of buildings may be reliable, but not very relevant, especially if they were purchased "long ago." Thus, having both relevance and reliability, although a worthy goal, is often difficult to achieve.

The audit profession helps to ensure some measure of reliability. However, auditors do not certify or guarantee the accuracy of the Financial Statements and notes. In fact, given the complexity of corporations, it is quite likely that human error has caused some mistakes in the Financial Statements. Rather, auditors attempt to obtain "**reasonable assurance about whether the Financial Statements are free of material misstatements**" (emphasis added). This quote is a standard part of an audit report.

The audit report will also contain an opinion about whether the Financial Statements that are specifically covered by the audit report "**present fairly, in all material respects,**" the financial position of the firm. If the audit report uses such terminology, the report is called a "clean" report.

CONSERVATISM CONSTRAINT

The conservatism constraint is pervasive in many accounting regimes, including that of the U.S. Conservatism shows the worst-case scenario in order to alert lenders and investors about the downside of their investments.

Example of Conservatism: Contingent Losses

A contingent loss is an event that may happen and that may require the firm to make payments to another party. Probable and estimable contingent losses are booked prior to realization. For instance, if the firm is sued for damages, this creates a contingent loss, which, if probable and estimable, would result in the loss being journalized, along with a corresponding liability. A contingent loss is a type of an "unrealized loss," that is, one that is recognized prior to a cash payment. Unrealized losses are sometimes called "paper losses." These types of losses sometimes are subsequently realized, sometimes not. For example, assume that a firm is sued for $1,000,000 and it is probable that the firm will lose the court case and have to pay that amount. The firm would book the following:

Assets	Liabilities	Owners' Equity
	1,000,000 Liability	(1,000,000) Contingent Loss

Reasonably possible or remote contingencies are not booked, but are generally disclosed as a note disclosure. This accounting treatment (statement disclosure versus note disclosure) is highlighted below:

LOSS Probability	Estimable?	Not Estimable?
probable	**statement disclosure**	note disclosure
reasonably possible	note disclosure	note disclosure
remote	optional note disclosure	optional note disclosure

Probable and estimable contingent *gains* are not booked. This would violate the conservatism constraint.

Conservatism is often expressed by accountants in the following way: book losses early, but not gains. There are exceptions (of course), and we will cover these later.

Example of Conservatism: Expensing IP Costs

Other examples of conservatism pertain to Research and Development Expense (R&D), which is the cost associated with inventive activity, as well as Advertising Expense.

Both R&D and advertising are recorded as expenses when incurred.

example

A firm spends $1,000 each on R&D and advertising. The firm would record the expenses as follows:

Assets	Liabilities	Owners' Equity
(1,000) Cash		(1,000) R&D Expense
(1,000) Cash		(1,000) Advertising Expense

Both R&D and advertising are "intellectual property" (IP) expenses. IP is an idea, and expenditures on an idea (that is, in effect, expenditures on people, the source of all ideas) are expensed, rather than capitalized. (Some R&D is in fact capitalized, but the threshold for capitalizing R&D Expense is rather high, so most R&D is expensed. We cover this topic in a later chapter.)

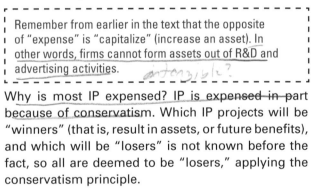

Remember from earlier in the text that the opposite of "expense" is "capitalize" (increase an asset). In other words, firms cannot form assets out of R&D and advertising activities. *intangible?*

Why is most IP expensed? IP is expensed in part because of conservatism. Which IP projects will be "winners" (that is, result in assets, or future benefits), and which will be "losers" is not known before the fact, so all are deemed to be "losers," applying the conservatism principle.

Conservatism introduces asymmetry in accounting, and invites the following questions:

- *Is it not important to let lenders and investors know about the upside, as well as the downside?*

- *Why do we have conservatism?*

We have no convincing answers, especially to the second question, which is, in some sense, a question about human nature. Indeed, why book the bad news prior to realization, but not the good news? Some have attempted to answer the question by drawing on psychology, but we will leave that to others.

ALTERNATIVE ACCOUNTING SYSTEMS: CASH, ACCRUAL, AND FAIR VALUE

The SEC, through the FASB, requires publicly-traded firms to use the accrual accounting system. The main reason for this requirement is that the accrual system better predicts future cash flows. Cash accounting records only cash events. It is typically used by small firms that may have only a single owner. Its purpose is to track past cash flows. The accrual system recognizes cash events and non-cash events. It recognizes revenues and expenses in advance of cash receipts and cash payments by setting up receivables for the revenues and payables for the expenses. The receivables and payables have future cash inflows and outflows, respectively, imbedded in them. That is, inside a receivable is a probable cash inflow, and inside a payable is a probable cash outflow.

```
A BIT OF PERSPECTIVE

Have you noticed the introduction of more uncertainty
recently? We have used the words "probable" and
"usually" more frequently as we wade through the
theoretical issues. Because accounting is a man made
set of rules there are inconsistencies and exceptions.
Don't worry, even the accounting experts cannot agree
on everything. However, this challenge highlights why it is
important to learn the concepts of accounting rather than
memorize the individual rules.
```

As we have seen, accrual accounting is based primarily upon the twin principles of Revenue Recognition and Matching. Revenues are recognized when earned and realized or realizable. Expenses are recognized in the period in which associated revenues are earned. Revenues cannot be booked without booking expenses, and expenses are not booked without associated revenues.

Conservatism is a principle of the accrual system that introduces asymmetry in the accounting system because it requires the recognition of certain losses prior to realization (unrealized losses), but it generally does not allow the recognition of similar unrealized gains.

There are other accounting systems. By way of introduction, let's consider the fair value system.

◀Fair value accounting▶ is an accounting system that is "bolted on" to the accrual system. Above, we saw where a firm recognized an unrealized, contingent loss. The fair value system requires recognition of unrealized losses and unrealized gains, but only for certain select assets and liabilities. Thus, fair value accounting violates the conservatism principle. It is a "non-transactions based" system since the gains and losses are from changes in values, not from transactions with independent parties. Fair value accounting applies to multiple classes of assets, and firms have the option to apply it to certain classes of liabilities. Also called ◀mark-to-market accounting▶ it is extremely controversial. The purpose of fair value accounting is to show current market values, because these are deemed relevant, even though they may not be very reliable and even though their recognition may violate the conservatism principle.

example

Assume a firm buys an investment for $100. Assume the investment is the stock of another company. Subsequently, the stock price of the investment goes from $100 to $120. Under fair value accounting, the firm would book the investment and the subsequent change in value as follows.

Assets	Liabilities	Owners' Equity
100 Investment (100) Cash		
20 Investment		20 Unrealized Gain

Thus, we see that there are instances when gains are recognized, in violation of the conservatism principle. We return to mark-to-market accounting in a later chapter.

```
DO YOU LIKE POLITICS?

Mark-to-market accounting was especially controversial
in the financial crisis of 2008. Politicians were critical of
mark-to-market for its lack of reliability and even mounted a
movement to eliminate this type of accounting. Proponents
of this approach support it largely because of relevance in
analyzing the financial condition of a firm. Controversies like
this have existed for a while and will continue to exist so
long as there is a conflict between relevance and reliability.
```

The main point is that we have a "mixed attribute" accounting model, since we use the above accounting systems simultaneously. Some call it apples and oranges, or "fruit salad."

EARNINGS PER SHARE: BASIC VERSUS DILUTED

When firms disclose their financial results, one of the key measures they announce is ◀**Earnings Per Share (EPS)**▶. Often the initial announcement of EPS (simply called "earnings announcement") is a press conference where the Chief Executive Officer (CEO), Chief Financial Officer (CFO), and other managers speak via conference call to analysts, investors, and other interested parties. Most large firms give the dates for their earnings announcements on their websites. They also often provide instructions for being on the conference call.

The interest in EPS is largely driven by the fact that it has become one of the major measures of a firm's success. The announced EPS is benchmarked against prior EPS for the firm and against the EPS of competitor firms. As suggested by the name, EPS captures the earnings attributable to each shareholder. Firms are required however to give two EPS measures, so-called "Basic" and "Diluted." ◀**Basic EPS**▶ essentially measures the earnings attributable to each existing shareholder, and ◀**Diluted EPS**▶ measures the earnings attributable not only to existing shareholders but also to those who could become shareholders by exercising their rights to do so. These differences are explained further below.

$$\text{Basic EPS} = \frac{\text{Net Income}}{\text{Average number of shares of stock outstanding}}$$

$$\text{Diluted EPS} = \frac{\text{Adjusted Net Income}}{\text{Adjusted average number of shares of stock outstanding}}$$

One of the main adjustments to the denominator for Diluted EPS is for stock options. People who hold stock options have the right to purchase shares of stock at a predetermined price, called the option price or the ◀**strike price**▶. They do not own the stock, but rather they own the right to purchase the stock in the future. They will likely "exercise" the option if the strike price is lower than the current stock price. For example, if an option holder has the right to purchase a share of stock for $5 per share, and the stock is currently worth $20 per share, the option holder would be able to buy the stock at a discount of $15. Diluted EPS would be the earnings per share as if these potential shareholders were actual shareholders, even though they are not, because they have not yet exercised the option. Diluted EPS is lower than Basic EPS because Diluted EPS includes in the denominator the effects of the additional shares that could be issued from the exercise of the options.

Another adjustment to the denominator is for convertible debt. Convertible debt is a type of debt that could be converted to shares of stock. If the debt is converted to stock, then more shares would be added to the denominator, further diluting EPS. (We note briefly that if debt is converted to stock, then interest expense would be reduced. This is one of the adjustments made to the numerator of Diluted EPS. However, we will not cover this and other complexities further in this text.)

One of the goals of financial modeling is to forecast a firm's future EPS, both Basic and Diluted. These forecasts constitute stock analysts' "earnings expectations." If the firm announces EPS numbers that are above the consensus, expected EPS, there could be a positive effect on the firm's stock price. If the firm announces EPS results that are below consensus expectations, then the opposite could occur.

> **A WORD ON TERMINOLOGY**
>
> "Consensus" typically refers to all stock analysts responsible for "covering" a firm's stock. There are many services that compile these estimates such as First Call.

In conclusion, we note that firms and their analysts sometimes adjust reported EPS. For instance, if a firm announces EPS that includes the effects of a contingent loss (discussed above), the firm may provide both GAAP EPS and pro forma EPS, both basic and diluted. Pro forma means for the sake of form, or "as if." The firm essentially is removing the effect of the contingent loss from the calculation to show what EPS would have been if the firm had not been required to book the contingency. Firms are allowed to "clean up" earnings affected by these typically non-recurring items, but they cannot mislead the markets. They must clearly distinguish GAAP EPS from pro forma EPS, and they must show what they have removed from Net Income to arrive at the pro forma results.

> By "cleaning up" earnings for users of Financial Statements, firms are guiding users toward what EPS or Net Income would have been except for the "One-time" or "Exceptional" items not expected to recur in the future. Understanding a firm's sustainable EPS, EBIT, cash flow or Net Income is the key to many types of financial analysis such as corporate valuation or credit worthiness.

Example

Assume a firm has the following Income Statement that is prepared in accordance with GAAP. Basic EPS would simply be Net Income divided by the Average Shares Outstanding, or $0.18 ($18 / 100).

Assume that the firm has stock options outstanding that could add 20 shares to the denominator. Thus Diluted Average Shares Outstanding is 120. Therefore, Diluted EPS is $0.15 ($18 / 120).

GAAP Income Statement

Revenues	100
Cost of Goods Sold	(40)
SG&A Expense	(15)
Interest Expese	(10)
Contingent Loss	**(5)**
Pre Tax Income	30
Tax Expense (Rate is 40%)	(12)
Net Income	**18**
Average Shares Outstanding	100
Diluted Average Shares Outstanding	120
GAAP Basic EPS	0.18
GAAP Diluted EPS	0.15

Assume that the firm wishes to show what its EPS measures would have been if it had not had the Contingent Loss of $5. The firm would simply recast the GAAP Income Statement as a Pro Forma Income Statement, as we show below:

Pro forma Income Statement

Revenues	100
Cost of Goods Sold	(40)
SG&A Expense	(15)
Interest Expese	(10)
Contingent Loss	**0**
Pre Tax Income	35
Tax Expense (Rate is 40%)	(14)
Net Income	**21**
Average Shares Outstanding	100
Diluted Average Shares Outstanding	120
Pro forma Basic EPS	0.21
Pro forma Diluted EPS	0.18

The Pro forma Income Statement assumes no Contingent Loss. When the loss is removed, notice that not only is Pre-tax income affected (increased by $5, from $30 to $35), but also Tax Expense is affected. This is because the higher Pre-Tax Income results in a higher Tax Expense (from 12 to 14). Therefore, the removal of the Contingent Loss in the Pro forma Income Statement is partially offset by an increase in Tax Expense. The "net" increase to Net Income is therefore $3 (from $18 to $21). The main point is that the firm, although allowed to provide Pro forma EPS numbers, which we see are both higher than the GAAP EPS measures in this example, must be clear that these results are in fact Pro forma and must clearly disclose the item(s) removed from GAAP Net Income. These supplemental disclosures are frequently shown in a table called the "GAAP Reconciliation" table.

At this point, we have covered a good deal of methodology, terminology, and theory. Let's now proceed and drill deeper into different components of the three Financial Statements. In particular, we begin the current section (current assets and current liabilities) of the balance sheet. ◄**Current assets▶** and ◄**current liabilities▶**, collectively, are called working capital accounts. The first working capital account we consider is ◄**Accounts Receivable.▶**

Chapter 4: Working Capital

By way of brief review, revenues are inflows of assets resulting from ongoing (recurring) transactions. The assets "flowing in" are generally cash or receivables. Firms book revenues when they are "earned" and when they are "realized" or are "realizable."

Generally, if a firm is selling a product, it will book revenue when it ships the product. If the firm is selling a service, it will book revenue once the service has been completed. Thus, to have earned the revenue, the firm must generally have shipped the product or the performed the service.

Payment for a product that has been shipped or a service that has been performed could be immediate. These sales would be cash sales. We say that the revenue is realized. If the firm is not paid immediately, the firm will nonetheless still book revenue since the firm expects to be paid. This is a credit sale and we say that the revenue is realizable.

Firms can also receive cash prior to shipping a product or performing a service. This is called Unearned Revenue, which is a liability, because the firm owes the customer a product or service.

A firm cannot book revenues without also booking expenses. Expenses are outflows necessary to generate inflows (revenues). Some expenses are directly associated with revenues, such as Cost of Goods Sold. In fact, expenses that are directly traceable to revenues are called "direct expenses." However, most expenses "indirectly" produce revenues and are called "indirect expenses." An example would be Rent Expense. Without a building in which to keep inventory, a firm would not be able to make sales. However, Rent Expense is not directly tied to revenues, as is the cost of the inventory that is sold.

Sales of services will not have a cost of goods sold associated with them, since the firm is selling a service, rather than a product. However, service firms will still have expenses that are necessary to generate the sales.

For firms that sell inventory and for those that sell services, various types of operating expenses will be necessary to help produce revenues. These operating expenses, typically called Selling, General, and Administrative Expenses (SG&A), include salaries, wages, rent, insurance, advertising, etc. SG&A is a pool of indirect expenses and is often called "overhead."

Whether selling a product or a service, one of the most common transactions that firms make is a credit sale. We begin with an overview of some of the issues that arise when firms have delayed cash flows from customers.

TIME TO CHECK YOURSELF

By now the above introduction to this chapter should be a review. If you are unclear on a few terms or concepts, a little time invested sharpening your knowledge will pay dividends down the road.

ACCOUNTS RECEIVABLE

◀Accounts Receivable▶ are rights to receive future cash from a customer from a previous sale on credit.

A WORD ON TERMINOLOGY

Other names for "Accounts Receivable" are: receivables, trade receivables (where "trade" = customer) and trade debtors.

---

example

Assume a firm sells a service for $100 and the service has been completed. Assuming the sale is a credit sale, the firm would make the following entry.

Assets	Liabilities	Owners' Equity
100 A/R		100 Revenue

The accrued revenue is subsequently realized as cash, as shown below.

Assets	Liabilities	Owners' Equity
(100) A/R 100 Cash		

Even though receivables generally turn into cash, not all receivables do. When a firm sells to customers on credit, the firm is exposed to ◀credit risk▶, or the risk of not being paid. Credit risk must be measured and recorded. This is addressed next.

⋯ ASK THE ACCOUNTING GURU ⋯⋯

If you were to pay for an item or service with your credit card how does the firm accepting your credit card record this transaction? Credit card companies usually pay firms in cash somewhere between two and five business days after the customer "paid" the firm by using a credit card. Therefore, the asset that the firm records is a receivable to the firm (A/R from credit card company) when the firm accepted your credit card. When the credit card company pays the firm, then the receivable turns into cash.

ALLOWANCE FOR DOUBTFUL ACCOUNTS

◀Allowance for Doubtful Accounts▶ is an estimate of uncollectible receivables.

Firms are required to estimate the amount of receivables that they do not expect to collect from customers. The estimate is based upon historical experience. The Allowance for Doubtful Accounts is a contra-account that reduces Accounts Receivable to its ◀Net Realizable Value▶, or the value that the firm expects to realize as cash.

Net Realizable Value = Accounts Receivable – Allowance for Doubtful Accounts

---

example

Assume that a firm that makes a $100 credit sale does not expect to collect 5% of the sale.

The firm will book $5 in the Allowance for Doubtful Accounts as follows.

Assets	Liabilities	Owners' Equity
(5) Allowance for Doubtful Accounts		(5) Bad Debt Expense

When the firm books the Allowance for Doubtful Accounts, it also records an expense called Bad Debt Expense. Bad Debt Expense will typically be shown as another operating expense (part of Selling, General, and Administrative Expense).

The Net Realizable Value of the Accounts Receivable is $95 ($100 – 5).

ELABORATING ON "ESTIMATE"

A firm's management makes estimates based on all available information such historical experiences in collecting similar receivables, economic trends and specific knowledge regarding the firm that owes money. Obviously this is somewhat subjective. However, users of Financial Statements can count on the fact that a firm's estimate is reasonable and supportable in light of the known facts. Additionally, users can further rely on management's estimate because the firm's independent auditor has agreed with the reasonableness of this estimate and the estimate may be subject to regulatory scrutiny. However, estimating is not a precise science and, therefore, estimates will vary amongst industries, firms and management teams.

Subsequently, assume that this estimate turns out to be correct and the firm collects only $95 of the $100. Since the firm has $100 in Accounts Receivable, but collects only $95, the firm will "write-off" the remaining $5.

First, we show the cash collection.

Assets	Liabilities	Owners' Equity
95 Cash		
(95) A/R		

Next, we show the write-off.

Assets	Liabilities	Owners' Equity
(5) A/R		
5 Allowance		
for Doubtful		
Accounts		

When an account is written-off, the Accounts Receivable is reduced and the Allowance for Doubtful Accounts is reduced. Since the Allowance account is a contra-asset, meaning that it has a negative balance, adding a positive amount to it will make the balance smaller.

It is possible that a written-off receivable is later recovered. This means that the customer ends up paying after all.

Assume that the customer subsequently pays the remaining $5. The firm would first reverse the above write-off to re-establish the receivable, and then collect the cash, as follows:

Assets	Liabilities	Owners' Equity
5 A/R		
(5) Allowance		
for Doubtful		
Accounts		

Assets	Liabilities	Owners' Equity
5 Cash		
(5) A/R		

NOTES RECEIVABLE

interest

Some sales have long payment terms, allowing customers to pay several months after the transaction. Firms that have to wait 90 days or more to be paid often charge interest. Thus, they book a ◀**Note Receivable**▶, rather an Account Receivable, because the former charges interest.

For notes with a term of up to one year, so-called simple interest is common. Simple interest is calculated with the following formula:

Interest = Principal x Rate x Time **where the principal is the amount owed**

example

A firm sells a service or product to a customer who agrees to pay $3,000 in one year. The Note Receivable explicitly states a 10% interest rate. Both the interest and principal are due at maturity. The dates given below are assumed.

On April 1, Current Year, the firm records the sale and the Note Receivable.

Assets	Liabilities	Owners' Equity
3,000 Note		3,000 Revenue
Receivable		

On December 31, Current Year, the firm has its Fiscal Year End (FYE). It must accrue interest up that that point in time.

Assets	Liabilities	Owners' Equity
225 Interest		225 Interest
Receivable		Income

Under the Revenue Principle, the firm will accrue the interest on December 31, the fiscal year end, even though no cash is received ($225 = $3,000 * 10% * 9/12).

On April 1, Following Year, the firm will collect all amounts owed by the customer, both the principal and the interest.

Assets	Liabilities	Owners' Equity
3,300 Cash		75 Interest
(3,000) Note		Income
Receivable		
(225) Interest		
Receivable		

Notice that on April 1, the remaining interest income of $75 is recognized ($ 75 = $3,000 * 10% * 3/12).

ACCOUNTS PAYABLE

These are amounts owed to suppliers for inventory and other items. For every credit sale, there is an ◀**Account Payable**▶. The seller books the Account Receivable and the buyer books the Account Payable. Sellers and buyers are called "counter-parties" and their accounting treatments will be mirror images.

example

A firm buys $30 of inventory on account. The cost of the inventory to the seller was $10.

The **buyer** would record the purchase of inventory in the following way:

Assets	Liabilities	Owners' Equity
30 Inventory	30 Accounts Payable	

On the opposite side of the transaction, the **seller** would record the following:

Assets	Liabilities	Owners' Equity
30 A/R		30 Revenue
(10) Inventory		(10) Cost of Goods Sold

The buyer would make only one entry for the purchase of inventory. However, the seller would book both the sale for $30 and the cost of goods sold for $10.

SALES DISCOUNTS, RETURNS, AND ALLOWANCES

Even though firms often sell on credit, they may also offer discounts to encourage buyers to pay earlier than they ordinarily would. This is formally called a ◀**Sales Discount**▶.

Sometimes buyers return inventory within an allowed return period for full credit or refund of the selling price. This is called a ◀**Sales Return**▶.

Also, sometimes sellers will offer price concessions to buyers after the initial sale, in order, for example, to encourage the buyers to keep the product, rather than return it. This is a ◀**Sales Allowance**▶. We illustrate Sales Discounts, Sales Returns, and Sales Allowances in the below example.

example

Assume that a firm makes a $1,000 credit sale of inventory that costs $600. The terms of the sale are such that the buyer can take a 2% discount on amounts paid within 10 days of the transaction. The buyer must pay the full amount owed if it pays after 10 days. Also, the full amount must be paid within 30 days; otherwise it will be considered "past due." The shorthand way of describing such credit terms is "2/10 Net 30," or 2% discount on all payments made within 10 days and the net amount is due within 30 days.

Assume the transaction is booked on February 1, as shown below for both the buyer and the seller.

Buyer

Assets	Liabilities	Owners' Equity
1,000 Inventory	1,000 Accounts Payable	

Seller

Assets	Liabilities	Owners' Equity
1,000 A/R		1,000 Sales
(600) Inventory		(600) Cost of Goods Sold

Assume that after the transaction, the buyer returns half of the inventory purchased because it did not conform to its specifications. The buyer and seller would book the following transactions:

Buyer

Assets	Liabilities	Owners' Equity
(500) Inventory	(500) Accounts Payable	

Seller

Assets	Liabilities	Owners' Equity
(500) A/R		(500) Sales Returns
300 Inventory		300 Cost of Goods Sold

We see that half of the inventory ($500) is removed from the inventory account on the buyer's books, as well as half of the Accounts Payable. The seller reverses half the Sale, half of Cost of Goods Sold, and half of Accounts Receivable (A/R), and increases the inventory by the amount returned. However, notice that in reversing the sale, the seller uses a new account, called Sales Returns. This disclosure is important, since it tells investors how much of the sale did not "stick." If a material amount of sales is returned, investors may worry about the quality of the products sold.

Therefore, sellers will show, either on the Income Statement or in the note disclosures, material amounts of Sales Returns. Officially, Sales Returns are contra-revenue accounts. If sales were simply reversed, rather than using the Sales Returns account, information about returns, and therefore possibly about product quality, would be lost.

Assume that the buyer wishes to return more inventory. However, assume now that the seller offers the buyer a price break if the buyer will keep the inventory, rather than return it. This is officially called a Sales Allowance, which is another contra-revenue account. Assume that the amount of the allowance is $100. It would be booked as follows.

Buyer

Assets	Liabilities	Owners' Equity
(100) Inventory	(100) Accounts Payable	

The buyer simply reduces Inventory and Accounts Payable by $100 because the purchase price of the inventory has been reduced by the seller's price concession.

Seller

Assets	Liabilities	Owners' Equity
(100) A/R		(100) Sales Allowance

For the seller, since the inventory is not returned, there is no reversal of Cost of Goods Sold and no increase in the inventory account. However, the amount of cash that the seller will receive has been reduced due to the price concession. Therefore, the seller reduces the Accounts Receivable (A/R) and also books the Sales Allowance.

Finally, assume that the buyer, on February 8, pays the remaining amount due. Thus, the buyer would pay 98% of the amount owed because the payment occurs within the 10 day "discount window."

Buyer

Assets	Liabilities	Owners' Equity
(392) Cash	(400) Account Payable	
(8) Inventory		

Seller

Assets	Liabilities	Owners' Equity
392 Cash		(8) Sales Discounts
(400) A/R		

The buyer will pay $392. This is 98% of the remaining amount owed of $400 (400=1,000 – 500 – 100). For the buyer, the difference between the amount in Accounts Payable and the amount paid ($8) is shown as a reduction in inventory. For the seller, the difference between the amount in Accounts Receivable and the amount of cash received is shown as yet another contra-revenue account, namely Sales Discounts.

The three contra-revenue accounts provide information about product quality and consumer behavior. We normally check to see if there is a growing percentage of Sales Returns, Discounts or Allowances over time.

Usually the details about the contra-revenue accounts are in the note disclosures to the Financial Statements. The seller may sometimes show on the face of the Income Statement "Gross Sales." However, this is uncommon. Instead, usually we find "Net Sales," in which case the details about the contra-accounts will be in the notes.

Gross Sales Disclosure

Sales (Gross)	$1,000
Sales Returns	(500)
Sales Allowances	(100)
Sales Discounts	(8)
Net Sales	**$392**

Net Sales Disclosure

Net Sales	$392

Finally, we note that if the buyer pays the amount owed after the discount window, the buyer would pay the full $400 and would not receive a discount. It would be booked as follows:

Buyer

Assets	Liabilities	Owners' Equity
(400) Cash	(400) Accounts Payable	

Seller

Assets	Liabilities	Owners' Equity
400 Cash		
(400) A/R		

INVENTORIES

Inventories are items that are purchased (or manufactured) for re-sale.

◀Inventory▶ has been called a "necessary evil." It is costly to have, but whenever a customer wants it, it is costly not to have. Inventory is costly to have because it represents cash (dollars) sitting on the shelves, rather than in the bank earning interest, and it is costly not to have because the customer will go elsewhere.

Having the proper amount of inventory is a dilemma and usually covered in an "Operations Management" course. Having the proper Inventory itself (types, styles, models, colors, etc.) is another dilemma, and this is a merchandising problem. Anticipating what customers will want to buy, when they will want to buy it, and what price they are willing to pay for it are all keys to a successful business.

Managerial accountants are involved in the decision process, too, along with operations personnel and merchandisers and marketers. Managerial accountants often help source and price inventory from vendors. They sometimes are involved with the decision about whether to make a particular item of Inventory "in-house" or to buy it from a vendor.

Financial accountants' main concern is the valuation of Inventory for financial reporting. Proper valuation is important, not only for valuing the asset (the Inventory), but also for valuing the expense (the cost of the Inventory sold, or Cost of Goods Sold).

Manufacturers have 3 types of inventory:

- ◀direct materials▶ *(DM)* = raw
- ◀work in process▶ *(WIP)* = being produced
- ◀finished goods▶ *(FG)* = self explan...

DM is the raw material that goes into the product. It could be the leather, plastic, fabric, wires, string, etc. As DM is needed in production, it is physically transferred to work-in-process (WIP). In production, DM is combined with Direct Labor (DL) and overhead (OH). OH is also called "indirect manufacturing costs," to distinguish from the direct manufacturing costs, which are DM and DL.

A BIT OF PERSPECTIVE

Inventory compositions vary from industry to industry and by firms within each industry. For example, a services firm such as a law firm will have minimal inventory (if any) while a clothing manufacturer will have a one or two seasons of product at various stages of production. Contrast the clothing manufacturer with a satellite manufacturer whose product is so specialized that it may take years to build and deliver.

Overhead (OH) includes salaries, depreciation on the building and equipment, insurance, utilities, and other such costs that cannot be easily traced to the production of a specific product, but nonetheless are needed to manufacture the product. The completed product is transferred from Work in Process Inventory (WIP) to Finished Goods Inventory (FG). The dollar value of the completed product is called the Cost of Goods Manufactured (CGM). When finished goods are sold, they become Cost of Goods Sold.

The flow of costs through the accounting system is shown next.

Direct Materials Inventory

Beginning Balance	+ Increases – Decreases =	Ending Balance
	Purchases	
	(Direct Materials Used)	

Work-in-Process Inventory

Beginning Balance	+ Increases - Decreases =	Ending Balance
	Direct Materials Used	
	Direct Labor	
	Overhead *(production-related salaries, depreciation, etc.)*	
	(Cost of goods manufactured)	

Finished Goods Inventory

Beginning Balance	+ Increases - Decreases =	Ending Balance
	Cost of goods manufactured	
	(Cost of Goods Sold)	

Above, we show depreciation as a part of Overhead, which is a part of WIP Inventory. What this means is that depreciation on a building that is used in manufacturing is capitalized, rather than expensed.

For example, assume that a firm has $100 of depreciation on a manufacturing facility. The depreciation would be recorded in the following way:

Assets	Liabilities	Owners' Equity
(100) A/D		
100 Inventory (WIP)		

To capitalize depreciation, Inventory is increased for the amount of depreciation, as well as the contra-account, Accumulated Depreciation (A/D). This differs from what we are accustomed to seeing, which is namely a reduction of Owners' Equity for Depreciation Expense. However, in a manufacturing environment, depreciation is first capitalized. After the above inventory is completed (becomes Finished Goods) and then subsequently sold, it will become Cost of Goods Sold, which will include the depreciation that was capitalized. Thus, "capitalized depreciation" does become an expense, but not until the Inventory is sold.

For disclosure purposes, if the amounts of each inventory (DM, WIP, and FG) are material, manufacturers must show each one separately, either on the face of the Balance Sheet or in the note disclosures. Regardless of where disclosed, the information can indicate whether the firm is experiencing difficulties. A buildup of inventory early in the production process may signal production problems, and a buildup of Finished Goods could signal weak demand. For example, below are two firms with the same total Inventory but different Inventory allocations.

Firm	DM	WIP	FG	Total
A	100	10	10	120
B	10	10	100	120

Without knowing any other details, most of us would consider Firm B to have some problems moving its FG. The only way to sell the Inventory may be to discount the price, which will squeeze margins and reduce cash flows. However, on the other hand, it is possible that Firm B is building up Inventory for an anticipated seasonal demand, and the customers are not yet willing or able to take delivery. Firm A appears to be loading the production pipeline, presumably in anticipation of future sales, but there is not enough information in this simple illustration to indicate when production would commence. Alternatively, if the production process is shut down for some reason, then we would also see a buildup in DM. The point of the illustration is that such extremes warrant investigation and reading the firm's Financial Statements (the note disclosures and other such disclosures) would shed light on the situation that the firm is facing.

ASK THE ACCOUNTING GURU

Remember earlier in this text where we discussed that Financial Statements are a great place to start analyzing a firm? Industry data, competitor information or other market influences could be compared to a firm's Financial Statement inventory details to better understand how the firm is positioned in the marketplace. Pulling together different pieces of information and putting that information to work is part of the art of Financial Statement Analysis.

Measuring Inventory Costs when Prices Change: Specific Identification, LIFO, FIFO, Average

Inventories present an interesting dilemma for firms when the cost of Inventory changes over time, either through inflation or deflation. Assume a retailer has 1 unit of Inventory that cost $10. Assume that the firm buys one more unit of the same Inventory for $12. Thus, the Inventory cost has risen by 20% (from $10 to $12).

Now assume that the firm sells one of the two units. Assume that the selling price is $20.

How does the firm assign a cost to the unit that it sold and to the one that it keeps?

If the inventory items are particularly "special," then they will be accounted for using the ◀**Specific Identification Method**▶. In this method, the firm knows precisely which of the 2 items it is selling and can assign the appropriate value to Cost of Goods Sold. If it sells the first item, Cost of Goods Sold is $10. If it sells the second item, Cost of Goods Sold is $12.

Specific Identification is used for large, expensive, or "big ticket" items. Most Inventory, however, is indistinguishable. For example, assume the two items of Inventory are hammers. A firm sells a hammer, but it does not keep track of which of the two hammers it sells. What matters in accounting is not the flow of physical inventory, but the flow of cost. Firms have to be careful to track the values of the Inventory, meaning that they must keep up with the fact that they spent $10 first. Then they spent $12. The price tags, so to speak, come off the hammers, but they are kept in chronological order. When it is time to sell a hammer, the firm pulls a hammer off the shelf (it does not matter which one), and then it assigns a cost to it. Here is where the other methods are used.

The other methods for assigning costs are as follows:

- ◀**LIFO (Last-in-First-Out)**▶
- ◀**FIFO (First-In-First-Out)**▶
- ◀**Average**▶

Below we recap the data:

	# units	$/unit
Beginning Inventory	1	10 (cost)
Purchase	1	12 (cost)
Sell	1	20 (selling price)

LIFO stands for Last in First Out, meaning the cost of the second item ("last one in") is assigned to the product that is sold. Thus, under LIFO, the firm will assign $12 to Cost of Goods Sold and $10 to Inventory. FIFO (First in First Out) means that the cost of the first item in Inventory is assigned to the product that is sold. Thus, under FIFO, the firm assigns $10 to Cost of Goods Sold and $12 to Inventory.

A BIT OF PERSPECTIVE

LIFO is not allowed extensively outside of the U.S. and is prohibited under IASB GAAP. However, it is important to show examples of complications that can exist with inventory.

For the average, we take a weighted average of the two prices. Here, the weights are "1" on both units, since the firm has only one unit at each price. So, the average is simply $11, or (10+12) / 2.

Here are the values for Cost of Goods Sold and Ending Inventory for LIFO, FIFO, and Average.

	Cost of Goods Sold	Ending Inventory
LIFO	12	10
FIFO	10	12
Average	11=(10+12)/2	11

Notice that if prices rise, LIFO gives the lowest Net Income, and FIFO gives the highest Net Income. This is because LIFO has the highest Cost of Goods Sold ($12). The higher the expense (Cost of Goods Sold), the lower Net Income will be. The converse is true for FIFO. Average will give a result between the extremes of LIFO and FIFO.

Since LIFO gives the lowest Net Income when prices are rising (that is, during inflationary periods), and FIFO gives the highest, one might think that firms would want to use FIFO to measure Cost of Goods Sold in order to have high earnings. However, LIFO is allowed on the tax return in the U.S. LIFO is attractive for the tax return because it gives the biggest deduction ($12, rather than $11 or $10). If firms have large deductions, they have to pay less to the government in taxes. By law, firms that want to use LIFO for taxes must also use LIFO on the Income Statement. For this reason, we often see LIFO being used in inflationary periods (because it reduces taxes), even though it also reduces Net Income.

LIFO is basically a government subsidy (in the U.S.) for the effects of inflation. Other countries simply give a tax credit. In fact, in many countries LIFO is not allowed as an Inventory costing method.

Lower of Cost or Market

At the end of the year, after the inventory has been valued at cost, it must be compared to market value. One measure of market value is what it would cost to replace the Inventory at current prices. If the market value is below the cost (however determined, using LIFO, FIFO, etc.) then the Inventory must be written down. In this way, Inventory is carried on the books at the ◄**lower of cost or market**▶. This is another application of the conservatism principle.

example

Assume that a firm's ending Inventory, valued at cost, is $90, and valued at market, is $60. The firm will write-down the value of the Inventory in the following way.

Assets	Liabilities	Owners' Equity
(30) Inventory		(30) Loss

Inventory Errors

Sometimes, unfortunately, we hear about a firm that has intentionally overstated its Inventory in order to boost Net Income. An intentional overstatement is called fraud. This is how this particular fraud works.

As we have seen, the valuation of Inventory affects the valuation of Net Income, because when Inventory is valued, Cost of Goods Sold is simultaneously valued. If Inventory is improperly valued, Net Income is improperly valued.

It is sometimes useful to think about the Inventory costing problem in terms of the Inventory account, which we have replicated in the following equation:

> **Beginning Inventory + Purchases**
> **– Cost of Goods Sold = Ending Inventory**

In other words, a firm starts with a Beginning Inventory balance, purchases more (which increases the balance), sells some, which will correspond to Cost of Goods Sold, and then is left with an Ending Inventory balance.

Following the rules of algebra, we can re-write the above equation in the following way:

> **Beginning Inventory + Purchases =**
> **Ending Inventory + Cost of Goods Sold**

The left side of the equation above is called Goods Available for Sale (GAFS), which should be intuitive. A firm has some inventory on-hand and buys some more. Combined, this is the amount available for sale. GAFS is a fixed quantity. If more of this fixed quantity is assigned to Ending Inventory, that means that less is automatically assigned to Cost of Goods Sold (an expense), which would make Net Income higher than it should be.

Therefore, if Ending Inventory is overstated by, for example, $100, then Cost of Goods Sold is understated by $100, which means that Net Income is overstated by $100.

Let's now move further down the Balance Sheet and consider investments, such as investments in stock and bonds of other companies, as well as investments in tangible and intangible "fixed" assets.

Chapter 5: Investments and Long-lived Assets

In Chapter 1, we discussed firms' needs for outside capital. Firms can borrow from banks or sell their stock to investors as means of raising cash. In this chapter, rather than considering firms who need to obtain outside financing, we switch sides and consider firms who have "excess" cash and who wish to invest in other firms. In particular, we will focus on one firm investing in the stock of another.

CLASSIFICATION OF INVESTMENTS IN EQUITY SECURITIES

The accounting method for investments in the stock of another firm (also called equity investments) initially depends upon how much stock (as a percentage of the total outstanding shares) is bought. The accounting profession has arbitrarily decided upon three levels of ownership: passive, significant influence, and control:

- At *"passive"* levels of ownership, generally thought to be in the 1-20% range of ownership, the fair value method is normally used, although the cost method may be used in some circumstances (described below).

- At *"significant influence"* levels of ownership, generally in the 21-50% range, the equity method is used.

- At the level of *"control,"* that is in the 51-100% range, the investor consolidates the investee's financial results with its own.

> **A WORD ON TERMINOLOGY**
>
> With "significant influence" you may see "investments in affiliates" in financial statements. When there is "control" the investee is technically referred to as a "subsidiary" after a process called "consolidation".

In all cases (passive, significant influence, and control), at acquisition, the Cost Principle is applied. The initial value of the investment is its cost. If cash is paid for the investment, the investment is recorded at the amount of cash paid. Also, broker's fees are capitalized in the investment account.

We will cover the accounting treatments according to the above categories, beginning with the passive level of ownership.

PASSIVE EQUITY INVESTMENTS

For passive levels of ownership, occasionally firms use the ◀**cost method**▶. This means that the firm will not adjust the value of the investment on the Balance Sheet, but rather leave it at its initial cost. The cost method is used in those situations where fair value is not determinable because the market for the investment is not reliable. This method is not too frequently used because firms typically invest in stocks that are readily marketable. Also, going forward, given that the accounting profession is pushing for more widespread use of fair value accounting, we expect fair value accounting will one day be applied to these investments as well. If fair value is not easily determined, firms would have to estimate fair value of the investment with some sort of valuation model.

If the cost method is not used, the firm will use the fair value method. Under the fair value method, the security must be classified as a ◀**Trading**▶ security or as an ◀**Available for Sale**▶ security. Trading securities are bought and sold relatively quickly. Available for Sale securities are simply not trading.

···· ASK THE ACCOUNTING GURU ····

What is a "security"? The exact meaning of "security" changes from country to country because it is a legal definition. For now, in the context of investments, "security" means an investment instrument (for example, common stock or bonds) that is readily marketable (can be bought and sold relatively easily). If an investment instrument can be bought and sold relatively easily it is likely that a market value can be determined for the security. Be careful! In a different context, "security" can also be the collateral posted by a firm borrowing money. The firm has pledged the collateral (such as land or equipment) to the debtholder in case of default on the loan. The debtholder can seize the "security" in order to repay the loan.

Under the fair value method, both Trading and Available for Sale securities are re-valued to a new fair market value at every reporting date, *even if the value of the investment increases*, resulting in a gain. Even though this violates the Conservatism Principle, it is believed by many that fair values (current market values) are more relevant than the historical costs. Thus, relevance "trumps" conservatism in this instance.

If the investments are classified as Trading, the gain or loss flows through the Income Statement. If the investments are classified as Available for Sale, the gain or loss is held in the Balance Sheet in Owners' Equity in an account called ◀**Accumulated Other Comprehensive Income (AOCI)**▶.

example

A firm (the "investor") buys the stock of another firm for $100. The fair market values of the investment on each of the ensuing reporting dates are $110, $90, and $150. Finally, it is sold for $150. The data are summarized below:

Purchase Price	Market Values on Sequential Reporting Dates			Selling Price
$100	$110	$90	$150	$150

"Reporting Dates" refer to whenever the firm must assemble their Financial Statements. Public firms are often required to "report" their Financial Statements every quarter to the public. However, firms often assemble their Financial Statements more frequently for the firm's internal management to review. Some retailers "report" weekly and trading firms even "report" daily!

If the security is classified as Trading, then the investor will mark-to-market the investment on each reporting date. In this case, the journal entries for each reporting date would be as follows:

Assets	Liabilities	Owners' Equity
100 Investment (100) Cash		
10 Investment		10 Gain (unrealized)
(20) Investment		(20) Loss (unrealized)
60 Investment		60 Gain (unrealized)
150 Cash (150) Investment		

The unrealized gains and losses are temporary accounts and thus are closed to Retained Earnings. Unrealized gains and losses result from changes in values, not from transactions with an independent party.

If the firm classifies the investment as Available-for-Sale, then the firm would also mark-to-market the investment on each reporting date, but the unrealized gains and losses are "frozen" on the Balance Sheet—

they do not flow through to the Income Statement until the investment is sold. They are stored in AOCI, as illustrated below for each reporting date:

Assets	Liabilities	Owners' Equity
100 Investment (100) Cash		
10 Investment		10 AOCI
(20) Investment		(20) AOCI
60 Investment		60 AOCI
150 Cash (150) Investment		(50) AOCI 50 Gain

AOCI is a permanent account, meaning that it is on the Balance Sheet rather than included in Net Income. It is however terminated at disposition (as we see in the final entry above) in order to recognize the gain in the Income Statement.

AOCI holds a hodge-podge of items. Frankly, we call it the "trash can." In it are various mark-to-market related gains and losses that firms lobbied to have withheld from the Income Statement. That is, rather than designating certain gains and losses in the usual way and having them show up on the Income Statement and then transferred to Retained Earnings, they are shown directly on the Balance Sheet in AOCI, bypassing the Income Statement entirely. They appear on the Income Statement in the future, when the related item is sold.

···· ASK THE ACCOUNTING GURU ····

Other items that are shown directly on the Balance Sheet in AOCI are certain types of financial instruments that have been deemed to be hedges, some pension activity, and special types of foreign currency fluctuations. The preceding qualifiers of "certain", "some", and "special" are due to the complex rules governing each topic. These rules and the resulting accounting are advanced topics. Rather than invest time in the complexities of the rules, finance professionals should be aware that these changes to AOCI reflect unrealized economic gains and losses to the firm's economic position.

To recap, when the security is sold, the realized (economic) gain is $50, because the firm receives $150 for the investment for which it had paid $100. If the fair value method is used, and if the security is classified as Trading, the $50 gain is allocated to the

Income Statement over the 3 years. In the example above, the total $50 gain is a result of recognizing a $10 gain in year 1, a $20 loss in year 2, and a $60 gain in year 3 (+10 - 20 + 60 = 50).

If the fair value method is used, and if the security is classified as Available-for-Sale, the $50 gain is recognized in the Income Statement in the period of sale. All of the intermediate gains and losses are booked on the Balance Sheet (in AOCI) and are not recognized in the Income Statement until the investment is sold in year 3.

SIGNIFICANT INFLUENCE EQUITY INVESTMENTS

The **◄equity method►**, rather than the fair value method, is used to account for investments in which the investor is presumed to have significant influence over the investee. This is thought to be the case when the investor owns between 20% and 50% of the outstanding voting stock of the investee. Under the equity method, the investment is not marked-to-market. Rather, the investment account is adjusted up or down depending upon the Net Income of the *investee*.

example
Assume an investor buys 25% of an investee for $100. After one year, the investee reports Net Income of $20. The investor's share of the investee's Net Income is therefore $5 (25%*$20). The purchase and the subsequent adjustment to the Investment account are shown below.

Assets	Liabilities	Owners' Equity
100 Investment		
(100) Cash		
5 Investment		5 Investment Income

Notice that the investor does not mark-to-market the investment account. Rather, the investor adjusts the investment account for its share of the investee's Net Income. The offset to the adjustment to the investment account is recognition of "Investment Income," which will be recognized on the investor's Income Statement.

···· ASK THE ACCOUNTING GURU ····

Where is investment income reported on the income statement? It depends on the central activity of the investor and the investee. "Investment Income" from an equity method investment could be classified as "operating" (or "above the line") if the investor and the investee share the same central business activity. For example, a manufacturer investing in another manufacturer. Conversely, "Investment Income" from an equity method investment could be classified as "non-operating" (or "below the line") if the investor and the investee do not share the same central business activity. For example, a manufacturer investing in a bank.

CONTROL AND CONSOLIDATIONS

When an investor buys over 50% of the voting stock of an investee, it has reached the threshold of control. In this situation, the investor will not show an "Investment" account at all in its Financial Statements. Rather, it will show the investee's individual assets and liabilities that it has purchased. Specifically, the investee's individual assets and liabilities are consolidated (merged) with those of the investor.

example
Suppose that an investor purchases all of the below investee (titled "Sub" for "Subsidiary") for $80 cash. We have listed the "fair value" of assets and liabilities, because these are the relevant values for purposes of a consolidation. The fair values may differ from the values on the investee's Balance Sheet, which are called "book values." Fair values are typically determined by an appraiser.

Sub's Balance Sheet	Fair Value of Assets & Liabilities
Cash	30
Inventory	20
Fixed Assets	50
Total	**100**
Liabilities	50
Stock	40
Retained Earnings	10
Total	**100**

The investor would book the transaction in the following way:

Assets	Liabilities	Owners' Equity
(80) Cash		
80 Investment		

The above entry is the same as the ones we made when an investor bought a passive, as well as a significant-influence, level of ownership. However, in this instance, since the investor controls the investee, it is not allowed to show a "line item" called Investment. Rather, it must remove the Investment account and in its place show all of the individual assets that it is purchasing and liabilities that it is assuming. This is known as a **◄consolidation►**.

The consolidation entry would be as follows:

Assets	Liabilities	Owners' Equity
(80) Investment		
30 Cash*	50 Liabilities*	
20 Inventory*		
50 Fixed Assets*		
30 Goodwill		

From the investee

As we can see, the investment is removed and replaced with the individual assets and liabilities of the investee. Goodwill often results from a consolidation, as it does in this example. ◀Goodwill▶ is defined as the excess of the purchase price over the fair values of identifiable assets, net of liabilities. In equation form, Goodwill is:

> **Goodwill = Total Amount Paid –**
> **(Fair value of investee's assets –**
> **Fair value of investee's liabilities)**

Thus, Goodwill would be calculated as follows:

Goodwill = $80 - ($100 - $50) = $30

What is the purpose of goodwill? Why would an investor spend more than the net assets are worth (that is, their fair value)? (This investor spent $80 to buy "net assets" of $50, resulting in the goodwill of $30.)

The most common answer is that the investor will be able to exploit the "synergy" that can be realized by combining the two companies. Synergy may refer to greater purchasing power, better distribution networks, etc.

CORPORATE VALUATION

How much a firm is worth is a little bit of and art and a science called "Corporate Valuation". There are many Corporate Valuation techniques. The five most popular techniques are: public comparables analysis, acquisition comparables analysis, discounted cash flow analysis (DCF), merger consequences analysis and leverage buyout analysis (LBO). Training The Street's self-study "Fundamentals of Corporate Valuation" explores these techniques in detail.

Officially, goodwill is an unidentifiable, intangible asset. Goodwill is also non-amortizable. This means that the asset stays on the Balance Sheet at its original cost. It is not depreciated like tangible assets, such as Property, Plant, and Equipment. However, as we cover shortly, goodwill is tested yearly for impairment.

A WORD ON TERMINOLOGY

"Amortization" means the same thing as "depreciation" except that "amortization" is used for certain intangible assets and "depreciation" is used for tangible assets. Both are expenses to allocate the usefulness of the asset over the asset's economic useful life.

Unlike goodwill, there are other intangible assets, which are identifiable, and which are amortizable, which we address later.

LONG-LIVED ASSETS

Technically, assets are defined as probable future benefits to the firm, resulting from past transactions. "Probable future benefits" is another way of saying probable future cash flows to the firm.

Assets are classified as current or noncurrent. Current assets are cash and other assets that are used, consumed, or sold, generally, within a period of one year.

Noncurrent assets also represent future cash flows to the firm. However, the lag between the acquisition of the asset, say equipment, and cash flows to the firm from the use of the equipment may be longer (and less direct), when compared to the lag, for example, for Inventory, which is a current asset.

Noncurrent assets can be subdivided into tangible and intangible categories.

Tangible noncurrent assets are those with physical substance, such as land, property, and equipment. Intangible noncurrent assets are typically certain "rights" (and therefore lacking physical substance) and include patents, copyrights, non-compete agreements, customer lists, logos, and other such items. Like tangible noncurrent assets, intangible noncurrent assets also represent future cash flows to the firm. A patent, for example, grants the firm an exclusive right to produce and sell a product for a period of time. This right allows the firm to reap cash flows from the sale of the product without also having to spend cash to ward off competition.

Intangible assets are often classified as "identifiable," "non-identifiable," "amortizable," and "non-amortizable." Identifiable intangible assets are those that represent specific, known rights, such as the patents, copyrights, and logos. Amortizable intangible assets are those that have known, definite lives. An example would be a patent with a non-renewable 20 year life.

Non-identifiable and non-amortizable intangible assets would simply be those that are not identifiable and not amortizable. A non-amortizable intangible asset would be one with an indefinite life. An example is a trademark, whose "life" can typically be renewed by the firm indefinitely. There are no non-identifiable, amortizable intangibles, but curiously there is a non-identifiable and non-amortizable intangible asset, which is goodwill, which we covered previously.

At this point, we might be feeling a bit dizzy. The below chart will help organize our thoughts thus far.

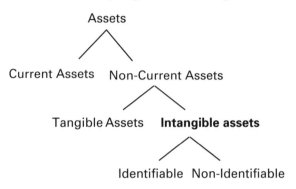

	Identifiable	**Non-Identifiable**
Amortizable *(definite life)*	Patents	X
Non-amortizable *(indefinite life)*	Trademarks	Goodwill

INTANGIBLE ASSETS

Intangible assets are generally booked when purchased. Assume a firm buys a patent from an inventor for $100. The journal entry would be as follows:

Assets	Liabilities	Owners' Equity
100 Patent (100) Cash		

Let's contrast the above to the situation where a firm develops a patent internally and spends $100 in doing so.

Assets	Liabilities	Owners' Equity
(100) Cash		(100) R&D Expense

As we covered earlier, the above treatment for Research and Development (R&D) and other intellectual property (IP) expenses is controversial. However, we include R&D in the discussion of intangible assets because there are exceptions. The exception to expensing R&D pertains to certain software expenditures.

Software can be developed by a firm for sale, or sometimes for internal use. Certain expenditures made to develop both types of software (software-for-sale and software-for-internal-use) are capitalized at various points. Costs associated with software-for-sale are capitalized once the software has been deemed to be "technologically feasible." All costs prior to this determination are expensed. Most costs are expensed under this rule, since the threshold for technological feasibility is high, and most costs to develop software-for-sale occur prior to that determination. Similarly, costs associated with software-for-internal-use are capitalized at the "developmental" stage. Subsequently, once the software has been implemented, the costs are amortized over the expected useful life of the software.

Generally, amortizable intangible assets are amortized over their remaining useful lives. Those that are non-amortizable (those without a definite life, such as renewable trademarks and goodwill) are tested for impairment, which we cover in an upcoming section in this chapter.

For intangibles that are amortized, the amortization would be done typically on a straight-line basis. For example, if a firm purchases a patent for $10,000 and the patent has an estimated economic life of 10 years, then the firm would book the amortization as follows:

Assets	Liabilities	Owners' Equity
(1,000) Patent		(1,000) Amortization Expense

TANGIBLE (FIXED) ASSETS

To record the acquisition of fixed assets, all expenditures to acquire the asset and to place it in service are capitalized. These would therefore include the invoice price, freight, installation, and trial runs.

Fixed assets can be acquired using cash, debt, stock, other fixed assets, or a combination of these items. If a machine's acquisition is financed with debt, it is normally booked at the present value of all future cash payments. (We provide a primer for present value in the next chapter.) This means that any interest on the debt is not recorded as part of the purchase price of the machine. In other words, the interest is expensed, rather than capitalized.

example

Assume that a firm buys a machine with debt. The present value of the cash payments is assumed to be $10,000. The firm will pay the bank $11,000 in one year for both the principal and interest, assumed to be 10%. The journal entry on the acquisition date would be as follows:

Assets	Liabilities	Owners' Equity
10,000 Machine	10,000 Note Payable	

The above transaction is known as a "non-cash" investing and financing transaction. The investing portion of the transaction is the recognition of the machine as an asset, and the financing portion is the recognition of the Note Payable. Such transactions are required as supplemental disclosures to the Statement of Cash Flows. That is, ironically, even though such transactions do not involve cash, firms disclose such transactions while discussing their cash transactions in the Statement of Cash Flows.

TRANSACTIONS THAT DO NOT INVOLVE CASH

Other non-cash transactions that you might find listed in a firm's supplemental disclosures to the Statement of Cash Flows include common stock paid to acquire another firm or an asset such as a patent. These supplemental disclosures are sometimes found at the bottom of the Statement of Cash Flows or in the note disclosures.

The machine would then be depreciated over its expected useful life. The note would be repaid, with interest, at maturity, assumed to be one year. We show the payment of principal and interest below to highlight the fact that the interest is expensed:

Assets	Liabilities	Owners' Equity
(11,000) Cash	(10,000) Note Payable	(1,000) Interest Expense

INTEREST CAPITALIZATION

As mentioned above, normally interest is considered an expense and therefore is recorded as a charge to Owners' Equity. However, interest is capitalized for assets that are built for a firm's own use. These are called self-constructed assets.

The calculation is similar to the calculation of simple interest. Simple interest is calculated using the familiar formula below:

> **Interest = Principal x Rate x Time**

However, to calculate capitalized interest, we use the amount spent (expenditure, as shown below), instead of the amount borrowed (principal).

> **Total Interest Expense = Principal x Rate x Time**

> **Amount Capitalized = Expenditure x Rate x Time**

> **Net Interest Expense = Total Interest Expense – Amount Capitalized**

example
A firm spends $1,500,000 on a project to build a building. The firm has total debt of $5,000,000. The interest rate on the debt is 10%.

Total Interest Expense	= 5,000,000 * 10% = 500,000
Less Amount Capitalized	= 1,500,000 * 10% = 150,000
Net Interest Expense	= 350,000

The journal entry would be as follows:

Assets	Liabilities	Owners' Equity
150,000 Building (CIP)*	500,000 Interest Payable	(350,000) Interest Expense

Often, while buildings are under construction, firms refer to them as ◀Construction in Progress▶ (or CIP).

The reasoning behind the capitalization of interest is that the $1,500,000 could have been used to reduce the debt to $3,500,000, resulting in only $350,000 in interest expense (10% * 3,500,000). The theory behind capitalization of interest is called "avoided cost," also known as "opportunity cost." The firm could

have not spent the money on the self-constructed asset and therefore could have alternatively reduced the debt, thereby saving interest.

It is controversial to account for "could-have" situations, but interest capitalization arose during the very high interest rate environment of the 1970s. Firms did not want huge interest charges on their Income Statements, and they were able to persuade the standard setters to allow interest capitalization. Thus, interest is on the Balance Sheet (in the Building), rather than on the Income Statement. The capitalized interest will be expensed on the Income Statement when the building is depreciated. That is, the depreciable basis of the building includes interest. Future depreciation charges, which will commence once the building is placed into service, will be higher due to the capitalized interest.

The total amount of interest, both expensed and capitalized, is shown in the note disclosures.

POST ACQUISITION

In the post-acquisition phase of accounting for fixed assets, the following events may occur:

- *repairs and maintenance (ordinary and extraordinary)*
- *depreciation*
- *restructuring (employee severance)*
- *impairments (lower of cost or market for fixed assets)*
- *disposition of individual assets*

Repairs and Maintenance

Repairs and Maintenance are the costs of repairing and maintaining physical assets, such as buildings and equipment. We have dual treatments for repairs and maintenance. So-called "ordinary" repairs and maintenance are expensed in the period incurred. "Extraordinary" repairs and maintenance are capitalized and then depreciated over time. Extraordinary repairs and maintenance are expenditures that extend the asset's useful life or increase its efficiency. Sometimes the distinction between ordinary and extraordinary is a judgment call.

example

Assume a firm spends $1,000 on ordinary repairs and maintenance. The firm would book it as follows.

Assets	Liabilities	Owners' Equity
(1,000) Cash		(1,000) Repairs Exp.

Assume the firm spends $1,000 on extraordinary repairs and maintenance for a piece of equipment. The firm would make the following entry.

Assets	Liabilities	Owners' Equity
(1,000) Cash		
1,000 Equipment		

The above amount that is capitalized in the equipment account would then be depreciated.

Depreciation

When a firm buys Property, Plant & Equipment (PP&E), the cost is capitalized. Over time, PP&E (except for land) is depreciated. The cumulative amount of depreciation is held in the contra-account, Accumulated Depreciation.

The difference between the PP&E account and the Accumulated Depreciation account is called the book value.

> **Book Value = Capitalized Cost – Accumulated Depreciation**

We point out that book value does not reflect true, economic value. It is simply the mathematical difference between cost and Accumulated Depreciation. Quite possibly, the asset (for which accounting requires depreciation) is economically appreciating. However, firms do not write-up the value (using mark-to-market accounting) of tangible fixed assets. Nonetheless, as we will shortly see, firms do sometimes write them down, when they are "impaired."

There are several methods of depreciation. The most common method is straight-line, which is illustrated below, followed by a brief description of two alternative methods.

example

A firm buys equipment for $1,200 cash. The equipment is expected to benefit the firm for 3 years. After 3 years, the firm plans to sell the equipment for $300 cash. This is known as the equipment's salvage value, or residual value. The firm will depreciate $900, or the cost less the salvage value ($1,200 – 300), over the 3 years.

> **TRICKS OF THE TRADE**
>
> Cost minus the salvage value is also known as the asset's "depreciable base" or "depreciable value".

On the date of the purchase of the equipment, the firm would record the following:

Assets	Liabilities	Owners' Equity
1,200 Equipment		
(1,200) Cash		

At the end of the first year, the firm would record the following:

Assets	Liabilities	Owners' Equity
(300) Accumulated Depreciation		(300) Depreciation Expense

The above depreciation method is called "straight-line depreciation." It simply divides the depreciable value ($900 = $1,200-300) by the estimated life of the equipment (3 years). This method gives an equal amount of depreciation each year. So this firm would recognize Depreciation Expense of $300 per year. Straight-line depreciation is the most commonly used method.

We will illustrate two other depreciation methods, namely "double declining balance" and "units-of-production".

◄**Double Declining Balance**► depreciation is known as an ◄**accelerated method**► of depreciation. Accelerated depreciation recognizes more depreciation early in the asset's life. The reason a firm may wish to book more depreciation early (and less later) is because as the asset ages, repairs and maintenance expense will increase. Larger amounts of depreciation expense will be matched with smaller amounts of repairs and maintenance expense early in the asset's life, and smaller amounts of depreciation expense will be matched with larger amounts of repairs and maintenance expense later in the asset's life. Thus, the expenses associated with the asset over its life will be evened-out.

Double Declining Balance applies a factor of "2" to the straight-line rate of depreciation. If the life of the asset is 3 years, the straight-line rate is 1/3. The double declining rate would be 2 * 1/3 or 2/3. This rate is applied to the asset's book value, which is $1,200 initially.

Depreciation expense in the first year would be $800, or 2/3*1,200. In the second year, the same rate of 2/3 is applied to the declining balance, which is the initial cost less depreciation recorded in the previous year. In this case, the book value is $400, or $1,200 − 800. Thus, depreciation expense for the second year would be $267 (= 2/3 * 400). However, firms do not depreciate more than the depreciable value, which is the cost less the salvage value or $900 ($1,200 − 300), and $267 would push the firm over the limit ($800 + 267 > 900). Thus, depreciation expense in the second year is limited to only $100. There would be no depreciation in the third year since the firm had reached the maximum in the second year already.

Don't worry, Excel has functions that we can use.

The Excel function for straight line depreciation expense is as follows:

> = sln(cost,salvage,life)
>
> = sln(1200,300,3)
>
> = 300

The function for Double Declining Balance (DDB) depreciation expense is as follows:

> =ddb(cost,salvage,life,period,factor)

where period is the year and factor is the rate, which for double declining balance is "2." Since 2 is the default, we can actually leave it out.

In our example, the amount of double declining balance depreciation expense for each year is shown below:

	= ddb(cost,salvage,life,period,factor)
For year 1:	= ddb(1200,300,3,1,2) = 800
For year 2:	= ddb(1200,300,3,2,2) = 100
For year 3:	= ddb(1200,300,3,3,2) = 0

Notice how Excel automatically limits depreciation in the second year to $100, the maximum allowable, as discussed above.

One other common depreciation method is based upon a different way to measure an asset's useful life. Above, we measured the life in years and estimated that the asset would be used by the firm for 3 years. It is also possible to estimate useful life in terms of "units of production."

Assume that the above asset is expected to produce 800, 600, and 400 units of a particular item over the next three years, respectively. The total expected amount of production is therefore 1,800 units (800 + 600 + 400). The firm would recognize depreciation expense of $400, 300, and 200, for a total of $900, calculated in the following way:

Year	Allocation for Units of Production
1	$400 = 800 / 1,800 * $900
2	$300 = 600 / 1,800 * $900
3	$200 = 400 / 1,800 * $900
Total	$900

The three methods are recapped in the below table:

Yearly Depreciation Expense for 3 Methods			
Year	Straight Line	DDB	Units of Production
1	300	800	400
2	300	100	300
3	300	0	200
Total	900	900	900

In all cases, a total of $900 is allocated to depreciation expense.

Earnings can be affected by the choice of depreciation method. DDB results in the lowest earnings early and the highest earnings later, because depreciation expense is larger in the early years and smaller in the later years.

····· ASK THE ACCOUNTING GURU ·····

Who chooses the depreciation method for a firm? Management of the firm chooses the depreciation methods. Management's choices, however, must be consistent and reasonably match the wear and tear on the asset experienced by the firm while utilizing the asset. Further, management cannot arbitrarily switch from one method to another method and changes are subject to the scrutiny of the firm's independent auditors. If management decides to change a method, the change must be discussed in the firm's note disclosures.

There is another important point about depreciation. Although above we show depreciation as an expense and have given it the title of "Depreciation Expense," sometimes depreciation is lumped together with other SG&A Expenses and given that title directly. To illustrate, we repeat our earlier journal entry that recognized $300 of depreciation.

Assets	Liabilities	Owners' Equity
(300) Accumulated Depreciation		(300) Depreciation Expense

Some firms will use SG&A Expense instead.

Assets	Liabilities	Owners' Equity
(300) Accumulated Depreciation		(300) SG&A Expense

Finally, we are reminded that some depreciation may be capitalized as part of inventory. Earlier, we showed how depreciation on a building that is used in manufacturing is capitalized. In that case, manufacturing related depreciation will become an expense when the inventory is sold. Thus, depreciation will be part of Cost of Goods Sold (COGS).

For example, if the above equipment had been used in a manufacturing environment, the firm would have recorded depreciation in the following way:

Assets	Liabilities	Owners' Equity
(300) A/D		
300 Inventory		

TIP FOR FINANCIAL MODELING

Identification of a firm's depreciation expense is an important part of building a financial model. Since it is a "non-cash" expense it is often added back to a firm's earnings when calculating cash flow. When you build a financial model remember that depreciation expense could be located in SG&A Expense or COGS or both! How will you know? Look for amounts located on the Income Statement and compare these amounts with what you find on the Statement of Cash Flows which always includes the firm's total depreciation (SG&A and COGS). (We cover the Statement of Cash Flows in detail in an upcoming chapter.) Finally, reconcile your knowledge with the Property, Plant and Equipment and the Cost of Goods Sold note disclosures. Learning how to manage the conflicting and incomplete information is part of the art of financial statement analysis and modeling.

RESTRUCTURING

‹Restructurings› pertain mainly to severance pay for employees that are being "terminated." We include restructurings here because they are often related to long-lived assets, and we wish to contrast restructurings with impairments which we cover next. Also, it is not unusual to observe restructurings and impairments occurring simultaneously at firms that are encountering difficulties.

When firms decide to undergo a "headcount reduction" or a restructuring, they must estimate the cash flows associated with the restructuring and recognize a Restructuring Expense, as illustrated below:

example

Assume a firm announces a restructuring plan and surveys employees to estimate the number of those accepting a severance package. The total amount of the restructuring cost is estimated to be $1,000,000. The journal entries to record the Restructuring Expense and to liquidate the Restructuring Liability would be as follows:

Assets	Liabilities	Owners' Equity
	1,000,000 Restructuring Liability	(1,000,000) Restructuring Expense
(1,000,000) Cash	(1,000,000) Restructuring Liability	

Restructuring expenses can also relate to other types of events. For example, a firm may need to terminate a lease for property. The expenses (penalties, etc.) associated with terminating the lease contract would also be a type of restructuring expense.

> **A WORD ON TERMINOLOGY**
>
> "Restructuring" is a "non-GAAP term". That is, the term "restructuring" is not listed in most GAAPs. Therefore, when firms use the term "restructuring" it can mean different things to different firms. When investigating a firm's "restructuring" charges you might discover expenses for writing down inventory balances to market value, losses on service contracts (where the firm suddenly forecasts that it will have a loss in fulfilling its obligation to a customer, (such as a fixed cost contract to build a road for a customer), and impairment.

IMPAIRMENTS

‹Impairments› occur generally when the future benefits that the firm expected to realize from its investment in an asset are in fact not being realized. When this occurs, the firm must "write-down" the asset. Firms must periodically test long-lived assets for impairments. Even intangible assets are sometimes tested for impairments. For instance, goodwill is tested yearly.

Impairment tests are quite varied for different types of assets (intangible versus tangible, for instance) as well as around the world in different accounting regimes. However, the underlying idea is similar, as illustrated in the below example.

example

Assume that a firm buys a machine for $36,000 and makes the following entry:

Assets	Liabilities	Owners' Equity
(36,000) Cash		
36,000 Machine		

Assume that the firm uses straight-line depreciation over two years with no residual value. The first year's depreciation would be recorded as follows:

Assets	Liabilities	Owners' Equity
(18,000) Accumulated Depreciation		(18,000) Depreciation Expense

At the end of the first year, the firm estimates that the machine's value has diminished because of changes in the economy. For example, the machine may have produced a product for which demand has significantly fallen. Thus, the firm will not be able to sell as many products, or will have to cut the selling price, or both. Regardless, the value of the machine to the firm is not as great as it was when the firm purchased it.

Assume that the firm estimates that the fair value of the machine, given the reduced demand for the product it produces, is only $14,000. However, the book value of the machine is $18,000 (which is calculated as the $36,000 cost less the above Accumulated Depreciation of $18,000). Thus, the firm shows the machine on the Balance Sheet at a book value of $18,000, even though it is estimated to be worth only $14,000.

The impairment loss is the difference between the book value and the estimated fair value.

Impairment loss = 18,000 – 14,000 = 4,000

To record the impairment, the firm would make the following journal entry:

Assets	Liabilities	Owners' Equity
(4,000) Machine		(4,000) Impairment Loss

Once written down, reversals of write downs may or may not be allowed, depending on the type of asset and the particular accounting rules being applied.

> IASB GAAP allows the reversal of impairment expense on most assets except for goodwill. These reversals, which are often called "recaptures", are only allowed to restore the asset's book value just prior to the impairment charge. In other words, the reversal cannot exceed the amount of the cumulative impairment charges to date.

Generally, however, impairments are reductions of value that are considered to be "other than temporary," meaning that reversals are rare.

DISPOSITION

When firms buy assets, they assign an "expected useful life" for purposes of depreciation. However, firms often dispose of assets earlier than expected. If so, the asset is depreciated up to the date of disposition, and a gain or loss may be recognized upon the sale.

example

Assume a firm purchased a depreciable asset for $50,000. The asset had a $5,000 estimated residual value and a 5 year estimated life. Assume that the firm used the Double Declining Balance (DDB) method for 2 years and then decided to sell the asset for $25,000.

The book value of the asset at the end of the second year is $18,000, or $50,000 cost minus $32,000 of accumulated depreciation, calculated in **Exhibit 5.1,** using both Excel and the formula for DDB.

The journal entry to record the sale of the asset would be as follows:

Assets	Liabilities	Owners' Equity
25,000 Cash (50,000) Machine 32,000 A/D		7,000 Gain

The asset is removed from the books. The related contra-account, Accumulated Depreciation (A/D), must also be removed. The cash received is booked and the Gain "plugs" the entry. Economically, the asset is sold for more than book value.

Specifically, the asset had a fair market value of $25,000 and a book value of $18,000, resulting in a $7,000 gain.

EXHIBIT 5.1

	Excel	Formula	Depreciation
Year	=ddb(cost,salvage,life,period,factor)	= (Cost-A/D) x 2 x 1/life	
1	=ddb(50000,5000,5,1,2)	= (50,000-0) x 2 x 1/5	= 20,000
2	=ddb(50000,5000,5,2,2)	= (50,000-20,000) x 2 x 1/5	= 12,000
Total			= 32,000

A BIT OF PERSPECTIVE

Some people think that if a firm sells an asset for a gain or loss that somehow the firm has made an error. The perceived error could be in a number of places such as estimating the salvage value, the useful life or choosing an appropriate method for depreciating the asset. These gains and losses are not an error. In fact, they are a common component of Financial Statements and are merely a reflection of the multitude of management estimates that are used when building the Financial Statements.

If the fair market value of the asset had been $15,000 instead, then a Loss would have resulted, as shown below:

Assets	Liabilities	Owners' Equity
15,000 Cash		(3,000) Loss
(50,000) Machine		
32,000 A/D		

We now turn to the "right side" of the Balance Sheet and consider Long-term Liabilities and Owners' Equity.

Chapter 6: Long-term Liabilities and Owners' Equity

Long Term Liabilities are essentially liabilities that will be paid after one year. They include Long-term Debt, Pension and Healthcare Obligations, Leases, Bonds, and Deferred Tax Liabilities, among others.

Many long-term liabilities are measured at the present value of required cash payments. Because present value is so central to the discussion of long-term liabilities, we first give a short primer.

PRESENT VALUE PRIMER

As implied by the name, **present value** is the value of cash today. For instance, $100 today is worth $100. However, cash has "time value," which we call interest. This $100 can earn interest and grow. For instance, suppose we deposit the money in a bank that pays 10% per year on all deposits. (The $100 is also called the principal.) After 1 year, the $100 has grown by $10, which corresponds to the amount of interest earned. The formula for calculating interest is:

Interest = **Principal x Rate x Time**
    = **100 x 10% x 1 year**
    = **10**

Now we have $100 in the bank. If we leave the total amount in the bank another year, it will then earn $11 in interest.

Interest for Year 2   = **110 x 10% x 1**
    = **11**

Now we have $121 in the bank ($100 + 10 + 11).

Notice that during the second year, we have earned interest, not only on the original principal, but also on the interest earned in the previous year. This is called **compound interest**, or interest earned on principal and interest.

The total value that we calculated (principal plus the interest earned to date, or $121) is called the **future value** of $100.

A BIT OF PERSPECTIVE

Present value has many applications outside of accounting. For example, present value is used in discounted cash flow techniques for corporate valuation. Although this primer is oriented around accounting applications, you might find that techniques learned or refreshed here will be helpful in many applications across finance.

We can derive a formula for calculating the future value of a principal.

Future Value at the end of Year 1:
= Principal + Interest for the first year
= 100 + (100 x 0.1)

The above can be rewritten in the following way:
= 100 x (1+0.1)

We can generalize the above expression as follows:

Future Value at the end of Year 1:
= Principal x (1+interest rate)

We can extend the formula for the second year.

Future Value at the end of Year 2:
= Principal + Interest for the first year + Interest for the second year

= 100 + (100 x 0.1) + (100 x 1.1 x .1)

The above can be rewritten in the following way:

= 100x((1+.1) x (1+.1))

= 100x(1+.1)^2

We can carry the algebra forward for multiple years but our "proof by example" can in fact be generalized such that the future value of a single principal can be calculated as:

> **Future Value = Principal x (1 + interest rate)$^{\text{# of years*}}$**

*or compound periods

For our immediate purposes of measuring and recognizing liabilities (as well as some assets), we need present value, rather than future value. Thus, the relevant question for our purposes is: What principal would be required today (present value) to grow to the value of $121 in 2 years, assuming the bank pays interest of 10% per year? We know the answer, since it was the starting point above (100). That is, we would need to deposit $100 today at the bank in order to have $121 in 2 years.

We can rearrange the above formula to solve for principal.

Future Value	**= Principal x (1+interest rate)$^{\text{# of years}}$**
Principal	**= Future Value / (1+interest rate)$^{\text{# of years}}$**
	= 121 / (1+.1)^2
	= 121 / 1.21
	= 100

Notice how the balance grows from $100 to $121 over 2 years. Such a growing balance due to interest is called **◄accretion►**. We can set up a table to show accretion in a so-called accretion table. Below is the accretion table for the $100 principal that grew to $121 over two years.

The table shows the growth in the principal balance over time due to the fact that the interest is being added (in the "principal adjustment" column). Further explanations follow.

Year	Cash	Interest	Principal Adjustment	Principal Balance	
		10%		100	present value (starting point)
1	0	10	10	110	
2	0	11	11	121	future value

Each row of the table (in this case, years 1 and 2), replicates the basic time value of money equation:

Interest = Principal x Rate x Time
(where the principal changes through accretion)

In this example, the calculation of interest would be as follows:

Interest = Principal x Rate x Time

Row 1:	10	= 100	x 10% x 1
Row 2:	11	= 110	x 10% x 1

The Principal Balance column is the sum of the previous balance and current adjustment to the principal, as indicated by the arrows in the accretion table, or:

For Row 1, 110 = 100 + 10
For Row 2, 121 = 110 + 11

Notice how the table begins with the present value and ends with the future value; the difference between the two endpoints is interest ($21).

As noted at the beginning of the chapter, we need the present value formula in financial accounting because many components of the Balance Sheet are measured as present value. For example, money owed to a bank is measured and recognized at the present value of the cash payments, as illustrated in the next two examples.

example

Assume that a firm borrows money from a bank. The bank requires that the firm pay back $121 in two years, which will include interest and principal. How much will the bank loan to the firm if it requires the firm to pay back $121 and if the bank's lending rate is 10% per year? We know the answer. The bank will loan the firm $100, which is the present value of cash payment of $121.

Present Value $= 121 / (1.1)^2$
$= 100$

When the payment of $121 is made at the end of two years, the bank will have been repaid the principal and earned its required interest rate of 10% per year.

example

Assume that a firm borrows money from a bank that requires that the firm pay back $121 in one year. As above, interest and principal are due at maturity, or in one year. How much will the bank loan the firm?

Present Value $= 121 / 1.1$
$= 110$

Thus, the bank will loan the firm $110. This will allow the bank to earn its 10% required interest rate.

example

Now assume that the bank expects not one, but two $121 payments from the firm. Each payment is due at the end of each of the next two years. How much will the bank loan the firm in this situation?

Now we combine the above two examples for the total amount of the loan.

That is, to solve this, we calculate the present value of each of the payments and add them together.

Present Value of First Payment $= 121 / 1.1$
$= 110$

Present Value of Second Payment $= 121 / (1.1)^2$
$= 100$

The total present value, which will correspond to the amount that the bank will loan the firm, is therefore $210:

Total Present Value $= 110 + 100$
$= 210$

Multiple payments that are the same amount and that are separated in time by a constant interval (such as one year, as in this case) are called **◀annuities▶**. We just solved for the present value of a two-payment annuity of $121. This particular type of annuity is called an **◀ordinary annuity▶**. It means that that cash payments are made at the end of the year. Ordinary annuities are also called "annuities in arrears." The other type of annuity, which we will not cover here, is called an annuity due (or sometimes, annuity in advance). For these, the payments are at the beginning of the year.

Earlier we set up a table to show the accretion of interest on a deposit of $100 that grew to $121 over 2 years.

We can set up tables for loans as well. Let's set up one for this example in which the bank loans the firm $210, requiring the firm to pay two, $121 payments at the end of each of the ensuing two years. The table is on the next page, followed by explanations.

Year	Cash	Interest	Principal Adjustment	Principal Balance
		10%		210
1	121	21	100	110
2	121	11	110	0

Each payment to the bank will cover part of the principal borrowed as well as interest incurred over the corresponding interval. For instance, the first payment of $121, made at the end of the first year, will cover $21 of interest and $100 of principal. Interest is calculated as follows:

$$\text{Interest} = \text{Principal x Rate x Time}$$
$$= 210 \times 10\% \times 1$$
$$= 21$$

The remainder of the $121 payment is the adjustment to the principal (100 = 121 − 21). In this case the principal balance is being reduced. The reason is that the interest amount ($21) is less than the overall payment ($121), thereby reducing the principal. When the principal balance is reduced in this fashion, the loan is an ◀**amortizing loan**▶. In fact, because the principal balance is getting smaller over time, we call this table an "amortization table," as compared to the earlier "accretion table" (where the principal balance was growing).

The first payment of $100 would be recorded by the firm in the following way:

Assets	Liabilities	Owners' Equity
(121) Cash	(100) Debt	(21) Interest Expense

Notice that the values for the journal entry come directly from the first row of the amortization table.

The interest portion of the second payment is calculated in a similar way:

$$\text{Interest} = \text{Principal x Rate x Time}$$
$$= 110 \times 10\% \times 1$$
$$= 11$$

Therefore, the principal adjustment is $110 (110 = 121 − 11), which exactly brings the balance to 0 at the end of the second year. Thus, the loan and interest are completely paid off.

Notice that amortization and accretion tables are constructed in exactly the same way. Both begin with the Present Value in the Principal Balance column and both end with the Future Value in the same column. The Cash column contains the annuity (if the problem has an annuity). The values for the Interest column are always from the formula, Interest = Principal x Rate x Time, where the Principal is from the Principal Balance column of the previous year. The tables are constructed so that "Time" is always "1." The Principal Adjustment is the difference between the Cash column and the Interest. The Principal Balance is the previous Principal Balance plus the Principal Adjustment if accreting, or minus the Principal Adjustment if amortizing. These relationships are shown in **Exhibit 6.1** below.

EXHIBIT 6.1

Year	Cash	Interest	Principal Adjustment	Principal Balance
		Interest Rate		Present Value
1	Annuity	= Previous Principal Balance x Interest Rate	Annuity less Interest*	= the above amount, plus (minus) Principal Adjustment if accreting (amortizing)
2	Repeat above	Repeat above	Repeat above	Future Value

*We usually construct the table such that these amounts are "absolute values", since these numbers could be negative, and we generally prefer not to have negative numbers in the table. MicroSofts Excel software simplifies construction of these tables. In Excel, to obtain the absolute value of a calculation, we simply put "=abs( )" in front of the calculation. In this case, the Principal Adjustment would be =abs(annuity - interest). We will see many more examples of these tables in upcoming chapters.

USING MICROSOFT EXCEL TO CALCULATE PRESENT VALUE

Excel is a useful tool, not only for building amortization/accretion tables, but also for calculating present value. Financial calculators are as well, but they all vary somewhat by manufacturer. We will illustrate the simple steps to calculate present value in Excel.

To solve for present value, begin typing the formula =PV( ) and then follow the prompts for the parameters, explained below.

= PV(rate,nper,pmt,fv,type), where:

- **"rate"** is the interest rate per year (or compound period, if different from a year)

- **"nper"** is the total number of years (compound periods)

- **"pmt"** is for an annuity, if the problem has one

- **"fv"** is for future value

- **"type"** refers to the type of annuity, which is coded as a 0 for ordinary annuity and 1 for annuity due. If "type" is left out, Excel assumes an ordinary annuity. If there is no annuity in the problem, "type" is irrelevant and can be ignored in the formula, since type refers only to an annuity. (Note that we are only using ordinary annuities so we can always ignore "type," since ordinary annuities are the default.)

example

What is the principal amount of a loan that requires a single payment of $121 in 2 years where the bank charges 10% per year? To solve using Excel, we would type the following into an empty cell in the spreadsheet.

= PV(rate,nper,pmt,fv,type)

= PV(10%,2,0,-121)

= 100

Notice that we input -121 for the future value because the firm will be **paying** cash. The answer is +100, meaning that the firm is **receiving** cash. (If we put +121 as future value, the answer will be -100. It does not matter what sign we put on which parameter,

but it is usually easier to think in terms of the flow of cash, either an outflow (a "-") or an inflow (a "+")). Also notice that we ignored "type," as explained above.

Example

What is the principal amount of a loan that requires two $121 payments at the end of the next two years, where the bank charges 10% per year?

= PV(rate,nper,pmt,fv,type)

= PV(10%,2,-121,0)

= 210

Again, from the firm's perspective, the two payments of $121 are cash outflows. Thus, we input the cash payments as "-". The answer is +210, a cash inflow, meaning that the firm will receive $210 in cash from the bank. Notice that we use the pmt parameter, rather than the future value parameter, as in the previous example. We use the pmt parameter because this problem contains an annuity (2 payments, rather than just 1).

With our understanding of present value of a single principal and of an (ordinary) annuity, we can consider various types of liabilities.

We will first consider Leases.

LEASES

A ◀lease▶ is a contract between a lessor and a lessee in which the lessor grants to the lessee the right to use property owned by the lessor. A lease contract is called an "executory contract," meaning that the contract is yet to be executed. In other words, upon signing the contract, both parties are bound by the contract and must perform the services and make payments according to its terms. However, just signing the contract does not amount to execution (performance) of the duties.

Most executory contracts do not result in journal entries when the contract is signed because neither party has fulfilled its duties under the contract. For example, a compensation contract, where an employee is hired and the firm promises a particular compensation in return for services, is also an executory contract. No journal entry is recorded simply upon signing the contract.

Since a lease is an executory contract, no journal entry is made at inception of the contract, unless the lease is a so-called ◀capital lease▶. It is so named because the lessee "capitalizes" the asset, even though it does not own the asset, and it also recognizes the lease liability (or Lease Payable). Both the asset and the liability are booked upon signing the lease, which is contradictory to the notion of executory contracts.

- -
A WORD ON TERMINOLOGY

A capital lease is referred to as a "finance lease" in IASB GAAP and in many GAAPs around the world.
- -

We explain why, after we first give the criteria for capital leases.

The lease is accounted for as a capital lease if any one of the following four criteria is met. Otherwise the lease is an ◀operating lease▶.

1. At the end of the lease, the title of the leased asset transfers from the lessor to the lessee.

2. The lease includes a bargain purchase option (BPO). This is an option for the lessee to purchase the leased asset at the end of the lease at an option price that is lower than the expected fair market value of the leased asset.

3. The lease term is 75% or more of the expected life of the asset.

4. The present value of lease payments is 90% or more of the fair market value of the asset at the inception of the lease.

The common theme throughout the above criteria is that the lessee is almost the owner. For the first criterion, the lessee *actually* becomes the legal owner at the end of the lease. For the second, the Lessee *probably* will become the owner since the lessee will probably exercise the option (since it is expected to be a bargain). For the next, the lessee is using up so much of the asset's life (75%), as if the lessee is the owner. Finally, the lessee almost bought the asset outright (that is, came within 10% of buying it).

Since the lessee is almost the owner in terms of receiving most of the benefits of the leased asset, then, for accounting purposes, the lessee is considered to be the owner and will show the asset and liability on its Balance Sheet. Notwithstanding the fact that the lessor is the legal owner, we say that the accounting treatment follows the *substance* of the arrangement, and not the legal *form* of the arrangement.

If the lease is classified as a capital lease, the firm will capitalize the present value of the lease payments.

example

Assume that a firm (a lessee) signs a lease contract that requires it to make annual lease payments of $121 per year for 2 years to a lessor. Assume that the leased asset's expected life is also 2 years. Thus, the lease is a capital lease because criteria #3 has been met. Also assume that the appropriate interest rate is 10%. This is the interest rate charged by the lessor to the lessee.

A lease is similar to a loan in that the lessee must pay cash to the lessor and the lessor also charges interest, just like a bank. However, in a loan agreement, the firm is receiving cash (principal) that must be paid back to the bank, along with interest. By contrast, in the case of a lease, the lessee is not receiving cash, but rather the use of an asset (such as property or a vehicle). Regardless, the lease will be recorded at the present value of future cash payments, just like a loan.

From the previous section, we know that the present value of 2, $121 payments at 10% per year is $210.

Below is the journal entry that the lessee will make at the inception of the lease (again, even though it is an executory contract:)

Assets	Liabilities	Owners' Equity
210 Leased Asset	210 Lease Liability	

Below is the amortization table for the Lease Liability:

Year	Cash	Interest	Principal Adjustment	Principal Balance
		10%		210
1	121	21	100	110
2	121	11	110	0

Below is the journal entry for the first lease payment, the data for which correspond to the first row of the above amortization table:

Assets	Liabilities	Owners' Equity
(121) Cash	(100) Lease Liability	(21) Interest Expense

The leased asset will be depreciated over the life of the lease, which is 2 years. Assuming straight-line depreciation, the leased asset would be depreciated by $105 per year ($210 /2). The yearly journal entry would be as follows.

Assets	Liabilities	Owners' Equity
(105) Accumulated Depreciation		(105) Depreciation Expense

The other type of lease is called an "operating lease." ◀**Operating Leases**▶ are more common than capital leases. Operating leases are called "off-balance-sheet financing" because the lessee is able to acquire the rights to use an asset without having to show either the leased asset or lease liability on its Balance Sheet. Unlike capital leases, operating leases are not booked at inception. The regular lease payments (rental payments) are booked as incurred. For example, if the above lease had been classified instead as an operating lease, the firm would book 2 payments of $121 each, as incurred.

These lease payments would be booked as follows:

Assets	Liabilities	Owners' Equity
(121) Cash		(121) Lease Expense

Lease Expense is typically shown as another SG&A Expense.

As a point of interest, the *total* (cumulative) effects of the two types of leases on the lessee's Income Statement are the same. If the lease is an operating lease, the lessee will record 2, $121 amounts for Lease Expense for a total of $242 (2*121). If the lease is a capital lease, instead of Lease Expense, the lessee will have Interest Expense and Depreciation Expense. The total Interest Expense is $32 (21 for the first year and 11 for the second, as we can see in the preceeding amortization table). Total Depreciation Expense is $210 ($105 * 2). Thus, the total Income Statement effects over the 2 years for a capital lease are also $242 ($32 + 210). Thus, over time, the effects on income are the same. These results are highlighted in the table below:

Year	Operating Lease	Capital Lease		
	Rent Expense	Interest Expense	Depreciation Expense	Total Capital
1	121	21	105	126
2	121	11	105	116
Totals	242	32	210	242

BONDS PAYABLE

Bonds Payable are amounts owed to bondholders. Bonds are contracts between borrower (the firm or bond issuer) and lender. In this case, we speak of the lender as being a bondholder or a bond investor, because they hold, or invest in, the debt of the bond issuer, the firm who needs to borrow money. (In Chapter 1, we distinguished between creditors and investors. However, we sometimes broaden the definition of investor to include not only investors in the stock of a firm, but also investors in the debt of a firm. Thus, we sometimes will call bondholders "bond investors." Generally, however, we reserve the term "investors" for stockholders. Bondholders are another type of lender to a firm.)

As we saw above with leases and bank borrowings, Bonds Payable are also measured at the outset at the present value of the required cash payments. Unfortunately, relative to leases and bank borrowings, the bond world uses many more different synonymous terms. The extra vocabulary can be confusing at first. The basic measurement, however, is simple, and we will save some of the vocabulary until the end of this section.

example

Assume that a firm issues a $1,000 "face value" bond that has a "stated rate" of interest of 10% and that matures in 2 years. The face value is the value on the face of the bond certificate that the bond issuer is required to pay the bondholder at maturity (after 2 years). In addition to paying the bondholder the face value at maturity, bond issuers will make periodic coupon payments to the bondholder. These coupon payments are annuities (for interest) and are calculated by multiplying the stated rate of interest by the face value. The stated rate of interest is a fixed interest rate that is also part of the bond contract. (There are bonds that do not require periodic coupon payments to bondholders, called zero-coupon bonds. We will not cover these types of bonds in this text.)

In this case, the bond issuer will pay the bondholder $100 for 2 years (at the end of each year) and then pay the bondholder the $1,000 face value (at the end of the second year). The $100 yearly payment (the coupon payment) is calculated as follows:

100 = $1,000 face value* 10% stated interest rate

Assume that the bondholder also happens to require an interest rate that exactly equals what the bond is paying, namely 10%. (The bondholder's required interest rate is the same idea as the banker's required interest rates on loans, or the lessor's required interest rate on leases.) More generally, this required interest rate is called the "market rate of interest," or the interest rate demanded by the market (the bond investor). It is possible that the bondholder wishes to have an interest rate different from the bond's stated rate. Rather than adjusting the bond's stated rate (which is already fixed on the bond certificate) we make adjustments to the bond's issue price. We cover this situation in an upcoming example.

Similar to leases and loans, to measure a bond liability, we solve for the present value of the cash payments. We discount the cash flows (the coupon payments and the face value) using the market rate of interest, not the stated rate of interest. We use the stated rate of interest only to calculate the amount of the coupon. The present value represents the amount of money that the bond issuer will get when it issues (sells) the bond to the bondholder (investor). Alternatively stated, the present value is the amount that the bondholder is willing to loan the bond issuer.

Using the standard present value formulas described at the beginning of this chapter, we would derive the present value as follows:

$$\text{Present value} = 100 / (1.1)^1 + 100 / (1.1)^2 + 1{,}000 / (1.1)^2$$
$$= 90.91 + 82.64 + 826.45$$
$$= 1{,}000$$

We calculate the present value of each cash payment (the 2, $100 annuities) over the ensuing 2 years, and the 1, $1,000 face value, which will be paid in 2 years.

Therefore, the bond issuer would receive $1,000 when it issues the bond to a bond investor.

In Excel, the formula would be as follows:

```
=pv(rate,nper,pmt,fv,type)
=pv(10%,2,-100,-1000,0)
=1,000
```

In Excel, notice that we input "-100" for pmt and "-1000" for fv, because the bond issuer will pay the interest and the face value (thus, cash outflows). Issuing a bond is really just like borrowing money. It has to be paid back, with interest.

The bond issuer would record the following when it sells the bond to the bond investor:

Assets	Liabilities	Owners' Equity
1,000 Cash	1,000 Bond Payable	

The payments of the coupons and the face value are below, again from the bond issuer's perspective:

Assets	Liabilities	Owners' Equity
(100) Cash		(100) Interest Expense
(100) Cash		(100) Interest Expense
(1,000) Cash	(1,000) Bond Payable	

We can also create a table as we did earlier with the loans and leases. However, in the below table, we are neither amortizing (reducing the principal) nor accreting (increasing the principal). This is because the cash payment exactly equals the Interest amount, meaning that there is no adjustment to make to the principal. (The face value of the bond is the principal.)

Cash	Interest	Principal Adjustment	Principal Balance
	10%		1,000
100	100	0	1,000
100	100	0	1,000

Now let's consider a slightly different scenario. What if the investor demands 12% and the bond is paying only 10%? Since the stated rate (10%) is fixed, we adjust the issue price of the bond. In this case, the bond issuer would have to lower the issue price of the bond in order to entice the investor to buy the bond. In order to calculate the issue price of this bond, we repeat the above present value formula, but this time use 12% (as the market rate of return), rather than 10%.

Present value $= 100 / (1.12)^1 + 100 / (1.12)^2 + 1,000 / (1.12)^2$

$= 89.29 \quad + 79.72 \quad + 797.19$

$= 966$ (rounded)

In Excel, the formula would be as follows:

= pv(rate,nper,pmt,fv,type)

= pv(12%,2,–100,–1000,0)

= 966

This bond is said to be issued at a ◀**discount**▶ and is recorded below:

Assets	Liabilities	Owners' Equity
966 Cash	966 Bond Payable	

In this case, we know that our table will be an accreting table. The issue price ($966) is the present value, which is the starting point for the table, and we know that the future value is $1,000. The ◀**face value**▶ (the principal amount) is also the future value. (We see the vocabulary creeping in. Face value is also the maturity value, is the future value, is the principal, and finally, one more new term, is also the ◀**par value**▶. Whew.) Thus, the face value is the amount that the bond issuer is required to pay the bondholder in the future (in 2 years). The accretion table is below.

Cash	Interest	Principal Adjustment	Principal Balance
	12%		966
100	116	16	982
100	118	18	1,000

Notice that the Principal Adjustment is added to the previous Principal Balance because we need to go from a present value of $966 (up) to the future value of $1,000.

The remaining journal entries that the bond issuer would make for this bond are, as before, for the 2 coupon payments and for the face value. These journal entries are shown below:

Assets	Liabilities	Owners' Equity
(100) Cash	16 Bond Payable	(116) Interest Expense
(100) Cash	18 Bond Payable	(118) Interest Expense
(1,000) Cash	(1,000) Bond Payable	

Notice that the Bond Payable account increases to the face value of $1,000 (from $966). The first 2 journal entries add $34 (16+18) to the Bond Payable account to bring the balance up to the future value of $1,000.

Let's do one more variation. Namely, let's say that the investor's required rate of return is 8%. The investor would pay more for this bond because the investor's required rate of return is only 8%, whereas the bond is paying 10%. This bond is therefore issued at a ◀**premium**▶. In similar fashion, the calculation of the issue price of this bond is show below:

Present value $= 100 / (1.08)^1 + 100 / (1.08)^2 + 1,000 / (1.08)^2$

$= 92.59 \quad\quad + 85.73 \quad\quad + 857.34$

$= 1,036$ (rounded)

Notice that we use the bond holder's required interest rate of 8% to calculate the present value of this bond.

In Excel, the formula would be as follows:

= pv(rate,nper,pmt,fv,type)
= pv(8%,2,-100,-1000,0)
= 1,036

This bond is issued at a premium and recorded in the following way:

Assets	Liabilities	Owners' Equity
1,036 Cash	1,036 Bond Payable	

Therefore, the bond issuer will receive more than face value for this bond because the bond is paying a stated rate of interest (10%) that is higher than the bondholder's required rate of interest (8%).

We know that our table will be an amortization table, because the present value is $1,036, and we need to arrive at the lower future value of $1,000. The amortization table is below:

Cash	Interest	Principal Adjustment	Principal Balance
	8%		1,036
100	83	17	1,019
100	81	19	1,000

Starting with a present value of $1,036, we need to subtract the Principal Adjustment in order to arrive at our future value of $1,000.

As before, the remaining journal entries, from the bond issuer's perspective, are below:

Assets	Liabilities	Owners' Equity
(100) Cash	(17) Bond Payable	(83) Interest Expense
(100) Cash	(19) Bond Payable	(81) Interest Expense
(1,000) Cash	(1,000) Bond Payable	

The cumulative reduction in the Bond Payable account of $36 (-17 and -19) brings the balance of the account from $1,036 to $1,000.

In conclusion, notice the following relationships:

1. **If the stated rate of interest < market (required) rate, the bond is issued at a discount.**

2. **If the stated rate of interest > market (required) rate, the bond is issued at a premium.**

3. **If the stated rate of interest = market (required) rate, the bond is issued at face value (which is also called "at par").**

Now, let's introduce a final bit of vocabulary. The ◀**stated rate**▶ is also called the coupon rate or the nominal rate of interest. The market rate is also called the ◀**yield**▶ or the ◀**effective rate of interest**▶.

In conclusion, we note that determining the amount of a borrowing from a bank, measuring a capital lease, and measuring the issue price of a bond, all require the use of present value. In each case, we discount the cash flows using an interest rate and time period. We can discount the cash flows individually using the formula (and add up the present values), or we can use a calculator or spreadsheet. Regardless, the main point is that these types of liabilities are measured and disclosed at present values of future cash payments.

DEFERRED TAXES

We now consider another type of liability (and, briefly, its counterpart on the asset side). This liability is one that arises from tax laws, which are enacted by the government.

Tax laws determine what items are taxable (and when they are taxable) and what items are deductible (and when they are deductible). Deductions reduce taxable income and thereby reduce the amount of tax that firms have to pay the government. The less the tax, the more money firms have for investing, paying wages, paying dividends, etc.

Sometimes tax laws require firms to postpone deductions to future periods. Conversely, sometimes tax laws allow firms to accelerate deductions to the current period, rather than having to wait to future periods. ◄**Deferred Tax Assets**► arise from the former case, and ◄**Deferred Tax Liabilities**► arise from the latter.

Specifically, Deferred Tax Assets represent postponed deductions, that is, ones that must be used in the future. An example of a postponed deduction would be a contingent liability or a restructuring expense. As we saw in previous chapters, GAAP requires early recognition of restructurings and contingencies under the conservatism principle, which requires firms to book certain expenses (or losses) and accrue liabilities before payment. However, the government would generally not allow a deduction until the liability is actually paid (sometime in the future).

One of the ironies of Deferred Tax Assets is that the *liability* for the accrued restructuring or contingency gives rise to a Deferred Tax *Asset*. The restructuring or contingent liability represents future cash payments, which may qualify as future deductions on a firm's tax return. Future deductions reduce cash payments for taxes and are therefore classified as assets.

Conversely, Deferred Tax Liabilities represent accelerated deductions. If deductions are accelerated and therefore used in the current period to reduce current taxes, future taxes will be higher. This is because the deductions will have been used up in the current period with none (or little) left for future periods. The higher future tax burden is reflected in Deferred Tax Liabilities.

Why would the government postpone some deductions, yet accelerate others? That is an excellent question, and it involves politics and governmental policy. Sometimes the government wishes to promote certain responses in the private sector, and it uses its tax policy to elicit those responses. For example, the government may wish to spur a certain type of economic activity, and it will give accelerated deductions to firms if they pursue that activity, such as invest in more Property, Plant, and Equipment or hire more employees. The large, accelerated deductions will allow the firm to retain more cash in the current period that it can use to invest and spur the economy.

A BIT OF PERSPECTIVE

Why would GAAP and tax policy produce different calculations for the same set of facts and circumstances? The two different systems serve two very different purposes. GAAP attempts to produce financial information that is both relevant and reliable to the user of Financial Statements while tax laws are a reflection of tax policy to provide a system for determining taxes to be paid to a government's treasury and promoting social policies.

The classic examples of activities that give rise to Deferred Tax Liabilities are purchases of depreciable assets, such as equipment, as illustrated in the below example.

example

In this example, we illustrate the effects of accelerated deductions and the resulting Deferred Tax Liability. To do so, we show the Income Statement separately from the Tax Return. Separate statements will highlight the difference between the expense on the Income Statement and the corresponding deduction on the Tax Return. (Earlier in the text, when we calculated Tax Expense, we did not have a separate statement for our Tax Return, because the Income Statement and Tax Return were identical. Deferred Taxes arise when the Income Statement and Tax Return are not identical and when the differences between the two statements are temporary in nature.)

Assume that a firm has $100 in revenues. The firm

also spends $20 on equipment that has a 2 year life and that will be depreciated using the straight-line method. Thus, the firm has $10 of Depreciation Expense on the current Income Statement.

However, assume that the government allows the firm to deduct on the Tax Return all $20 of depreciation in the current year. This means that the firm will not have any deduction on next year's Tax Return. The Income Statement and Tax Return are shown below.

	Current Income Statement	Current Tax Return	Deferred Tax Liability
Revenues	100	100	
Depreciation Expense	(10)		
Depreciation Deduction		(20)	
Difference between above Expense and Deduction			10
Pre-Tax Income	90		
Taxable Income		80	
Statutory Tax Rate (assumed)	40%	40%	40%
Tax Expense	36		
Cash payment for Taxes		32	
Deferred Tax Liability			4

In this case, the amount of cash due to the government in taxes is reduced by $4 because of the extra $10 deduction for depreciation. This extra deduction makes the firm better off in the current period because it saves cash that it otherwise would have to pay the government. However, in the future, the firm's taxes will be higher because the deduction is completely used up in the current year. The future higher taxes are the cause of the Deferred Tax Liability. The difference between the Depreciation Expense shown in the Income Statement and the Depreciation Deduction shown on the Tax Return is called a ◀**temporary difference**▶. It is temporary because there is a future tax consequence from accelerating the deduction. Although taxes are lower in the current period, they will be higher in future periods.

The journal entry to record Tax Expense and the Deferred Tax Liability is below:

Assets	Liabilities	Owners' Equity
(32) Cash	4 Deferred Tax Liability	(36) Tax Expense

Although the firm is better off in the current year because of the extra deduction, it is worse off in future years, because it will not have the deduction. In order to have future deductions, the firm could buy more depreciable assets, which is exactly what the government wants the firm to do.

Firms like the accelerated deductions, even though they give rise to Deferred Tax Liabilities. In fact, most firms would prefer accelerated (current) deductions rather than future deductions. Accelerated deductions mean that the firm saves cash "today." That is, rather than having to pay the government today, it keeps the cash which it can put to use elsewhere. Moreover, it is possible to defer the Deferred Tax Liability period after period, by continuing to invest in depreciable assets, which would "re-start" the deductions.

Before leaving Deferred Tax Liabilities, we should point out one more peculiarity. Unlike borrowings, leases, and bonds, Deferred Tax Liabilities are not measured as the present value of future cash payments. One reason is that we do not know what interest rate to use to discount the future cash payments, nor do we know when the cash payments will actually be paid. In bonds, for example, we have the interest rate (market rate of interest) and we know the repayment schedule, so we can discount the cash flows. Thus, among liabilities, some are measured at present value and others, such as Deferred Tax Liabilities, are measured at future value.

Let's now turn to our final section of the Balance Sheet, Owners' Equity.

OWNERS' EQUITY

Owners' Equity is the net book value of the firm (Assets - Liabilities).

CORPORATE VALUATION

A firm's net book value (sometimes referred to as "book value") is used for accounting and financial statement analysis purposes. Separate and unrelated concepts such as a firm's equity value or enterprise value are concepts used in "Corporate Valuation" and are more closely related to market values.

Owners' Equity is also referred to as the "residual interests" of the firm. What this means is that the investors (that is, the owners) receive the "leftovers" of the assets, after the firm's obligations (liabilities) have been satisfied, should the firm go bankrupt.

Owners' Equity has several stock-related accounts, described below.

◀Preferred Stock▶

Preferred Stock is a type of equity financing that gives the stockholder certain rights not granted to common stockholders. These rights include the rights to receive dividend payments before common stockholders. In addition, Preferred Stock ranks higher than Common Stock in terms of claims on leftover assets, should the firm go bankrupt.

◀Common Stock▶

Common Stock is the most popular form of equity financing. Common Stock does not enjoy the preferences of Preferred Stock. However, Common Stock does have the right to vote for shareholder resolutions and for members of the Board of Directors, whereas preferred stockholders typically do not.

◀Additional Paid in Capital (APIC)▶

Additional Paid in Capital is the amount of equity financing from investors that is above the stock's par value. Par value is a nominal value on the stock certificate. It has nothing to do with the market value of the stock that is sold. Par value previously represented the minimum amount of capital that investors had to put into the firm. Today, minimum capital is determined by individual states (in the U.S.) and individual countries.

A WORD ON TERMINOLOGY

Additional Paid In Capital is sometimes referred to as "share surplus", "capital in excess of stated value (or par)" or "paid in capital".

◀Treasury Stock▶

Treasury Stock is stock that the firm repurchases from stockholders. In fact, sometimes Treasury Stock is called Repurchased Stock.

Some reasons for treasury stock include:

* *stock repurchases may be favored over dividends by shareholders because stock repurchases can result in a capital gain to the stockholder which may be taxed at a lower rate than dividends*

* *stock repurchases counteract the dilution from stock options that are exercised by employees*

* *stock repurchases help boost earnings per share by decreasing the number of shares outstanding*

* *stock repurchases may be necessary to have an inventory of shares available for expected exercise of stock options*

* *stock repurchases may indicate management's belief that the stock is a good deal (implying that management believes that it is under-priced in the market)*

* *stock repurchases may preempt a takeover by another company that is trying to buy the firm's stock and gain control*

The balance of the Treasury Stock account is negative. Thus, it is a contra-equity account. Please note that purchases of stock of other firms are investments, whereas purchases of the firm's own stock are contra-equity (Treasury Stock).

example
Assume that a firm issues 10 shares of common stock for $10 per share. Assume that the stock's par value is $1 per share.

The journal entry for this example is below.

Assets	Liabilities	Owners' Equity
100 Cash		10 Common Stock 90 APIC

As we see in the above journal entry, the proceeds received upon the sale of the stock are split into two components, Common Stock (at par value) and Additional Paid in Capital (APIC).

Also assume that the firm issues 10 shares of Preferred Stock for $20 per share, and assume that the par value per share is $5. The journal entry would be as follows:

Assets	Liabilities	Owners' Equity
200 Cash		50 Preferred Stock 150 APIC

Most preferred stock pays a dividend, and the dividend is usually stated as a percentage of par value. We will assume that the preferred stock has a dividend rate of 6%. Therefore, each share of stock will receive $0.30 ($5 x 6%), when dividends are paid.

Assume that the firm does declare a cash dividend of $12.

Upon declaration of a dividend, the firm has a legally enforceable liability. Dividend policy is often determined by the firm's board of directors. Prior to declaration, dividends are optional. After declaration, they must be paid. The following journal entry would be made upon declaration:

Assets	Liabilities	Owners' Equity
	12 Dividends Payable	(12) Retained Earnings

Generally, the payment date is about two weeks after the declaration date. Upon payment, the journal entry would be as follows:

Assets	Liabilities	Owners' Equity
(12) Cash	(12) Dividends Payable	

The $12 dividend must be allocated to the stockholders. Preferred stockholders will receive $3 (10 shares x $5 x 6%). Common stockholders will receive the remaining $9.

Share repurchases, like dividends, are optional. Unlike dividends, however, share repurchases are not "declared." Rather, a firm (usually the board of directors) will announce that over a period of time (often a multi-year period), the firm plans to buy a budgeted amount of stock from stockholders in "open market transactions." Thus, there is no formal declaration of specific amounts that would require a journal entry. Rather, the firm will book the transactions only when they occur.

example

Assume that a firm re-purchases from investors its own stock by paying $100 cash. The journal entry would be as follows.

Assets	Liabilities	Owners' Equity
(100) Cash		(100) Treasury Stock

Later, the firm may re-sell the Treasury Stock. It is important to note that re-sales of the firm's own stock at prices that are higher or lower than the purchase price do not result in gains or losses. Firms may not recognize gains or losses on transactions that involve their own stock. Rather, firms will use the APIC account to absorb any differences.

example

Assume that the firm re-sells all of the above Treasury Stock for $120. The journal entry would be as follows:

Assets	Liabilities	Owners' Equity
120 Cash		100 Treasury Stock 20 APIC

example

Assume that the firm re-sells all of the above Treasury Stock for $80. The journal entry would be as follows:

Assets	Liabilities	Owners' Equity
80 Cash		100 Treasury Stock (20) APIC

Chapter 7: Statement of Cash Flows Revisited

We introduce additional issues and provide more examples of deriving the Cash Flow Statement in this section.

THREE CATEGORIES OF CASH FLOWS

As we have seen, cash flows are grouped into three categories.

- **◀Cash Flows from Operations (CFO)▶**
- **◀Cash Flows from Investing Activities (CFI)▶**
- **◀Cash Flows from Financing Activities (CFF)▶**

Examples of the major transactions within each category are listed below. Most of the transactions should make sense. For example, cash received from customers is classified as a cash flow from operations (CFO), since selling to customers is a major part of any firm's operations. However, a few of the transactions do not make sense. We comment on these below.

CFO

- *cash received from customers*
- *cash paid to suppliers, employees, insurers*
- *taxes paid*
- *interest received and paid*
- *cash dividends received*
- *cash received or paid in sale or purchase of investments classified as Trading securities*

TRICKS OF THE TRADE

In Chapter 5 we spoke about the "operating" section of the Income Statement where a firm would classify all of its activities from it central business activities. Unfortunately, "operating" for the Income Statement has a much more narrow definition than the more inclusive "operating" section for the Cash Flow Statement.

The peculiarities pertain to interest and dividends. It would seem more appropriate for the receipt of both interest and dividends to be classified as CFI. After all, both interest and dividends result from investing decisions. It would also seem more appropriate for the payment of interest to be CFF, since the loan itself (that is, the principal) is a financing cash flow. Finally, except perhaps for certain financial institutions whose primary activity is trading stocks and bonds, it would seem that purchases and sales of investments in Trading securities should be classified as CFI.

Regardless of our reasoning, U.S. GAAP classifies all of these particular items as cash flows from operations. Frankly, the reasons for doing so are not especially compelling and are not repeated here, but they can be found in the discussion section (appendices) of the relevant standards for those interested (available at *www.fasb.org*).

···· ASK THE ACCOUNTING GURU ····

Many items such as dividends and interest received or interest paid can be found in CFI or CFF, respectively, under IASB GAAP. While this may make more sense intuitively, it causes complications when comparing a firm reporting under US GAAP with another firm reporting under IASB GAAP.

Below we continue with the CFI and CFF descriptions:

CFI

*   *cash received or paid in the sale or purchase of property, plant, and equipment*

*   *cash received or paid in the sale or purchase of available-for-sale investments, held-to-maturity investments, and equity method investments*

CFF

*   *cash received and paid in short and long term borrowing*

*   *cash received from stock issuance, including the strike price from stock option exercises*

*   *cash paid as dividends*

*   *cash paid for the repurchase of a firm's own stock (treasury stock)*

A WORD ON TERMINOLOGY

Cash paid for the purchase of property, plant and equipment is often referred to as "capital expenditures". When analyzing financial statements or forecasting a firm's cash flows in a financial model, locating the "capital expenditures" and linking these past investments to management's discussion of future investments is part of the art of financial statement analysis and financial modeling.

LINKING CASH FLOWS WITH SPECIFIC ACCOUNTS

The process of deriving a cash flow statement is facilitated when we associate cash flows with particular Balance Sheet accounts. For example, "cash received from customers," which is CFO, is associated with Accounts Receivable. One of the changes in Accounts Receivable is this particular cash flow, as shown below:

Accounts Receivable

Beginning Balance	+ / – Increases and Decreases	= Ending Balance
	+ Credit Sales – Cash Received from Credit Customers (CFO)	

As another example, the Property, Plant and Equipment (PP&E) account can be analyzed similarly.

PP&E

Beginning Balance	+ / – Increases and Decreases	= Ending Balance
	+ Purchases of PP&E (CFI) – Sales of PP&E (CFI)	

The cash flows associated with both purchases and sales of PP&E are classified as CFI.

The cash flows associated with Notes Payable pertain to loans, which are classified as CFF, as shown below:

Note Payable

Beginning Balance	+ / – Increases and Decreases	= Ending Balance
	+ New Borrowings (CFF) – Principal Repayments (CFF)	

To extend the analysis to the entire Balance Sheet, we can group the accounts by cash flow category, as depicted on the next page:

Balance Sheet			
Current Assets	**Category**	**Current Liabilities**	**Category**
Accounts Receivable	CFO	Accounts Payable	CFO
Prepaid Expenses (rent, insurance, etc.)	CFO	Wages Payable	CFO
Inventory	CFO	Interest Payable	CFO
Interest Receivable	CFO	Income Taxes Payable	CFO
Marketable Securities – Trading	CFO	Unearned Revenue	CFO
		Current Maturities of Long Term Debt	CFF
		Dividends Payable	CFF
Noncurrent Assets		**Noncurrent Liabilities**	
Marketable Securities – Available for Sale	CFI	Long Term Debt	CFF
Land	CFI	Bonds Payable	CFF
Building	CFI	**Owners' Equity**	
Equipment	CFI	Stock	CFF
Other Long-term Investments & Intangibles	CFI	APIC	CFF
		Treasury Stock	CFF
		Retained Earnings	**CFO/CFF**

As we see above, most (although not all) Current Assets and Current Liabilities are CFO-related accounts. An example of an account that is classified as a Current Liability but is not associated with CFO is Current Maturities of Long Term Debt, which is associated with CFF. Similarly, Dividends Payable, another Current Liability, is also associated with CFF. Generally, however, Current Assets and Current Liabilities represent a firm's "working capital," and working capital is associated with the firm's central ongoing operations. Thus, it is helpful to view working capital accounts as, for the most part, being related to CFO.

Noncurrent assets contain those assets related to a firm's investments in PP&E, intangible assets, and other investments. Intuitively therefore, the associated cash flows are CFI.

Noncurrent liabilities and Owners' Equity contain the accounts related to a firm's financing policy, that is, the choice between debt and equity financing. The associated cash flows are mainly CFF.

In the preceeding schematic, we show that the Retained Earnings account is related to two different cash flows. It is a sort of "dual personality." The Retained Earnings account is shown below:

Retained Earnings

Beginning Balance	+ / – Increases and Decreases	= Ending Balance
	+ Net Income – Dividends Paid	

Dividends paid are CFF, which makes sense. The providers of equity capital are paid a return on that capital in the form of dividends. Net Income, however, is largely related to a firm's operations. As such, Net Income is associated chiefly with CFO. However, it contains many non-cash items, because of its accrual foundations. In upcoming examples, we illustrate how to handle Net Income.

DIRECT AND INDIRECT METHODS

Introduction

In earlier examples, we would derive the Cash Flow Statement by identifying individual cash flows in "real time," labeling them, and adding them up by category. Labeling the cash flows in real time is not done in practice. There are simply too many cash flows to identify and label as they occur. We will follow our old process one more time and then introduce alternative methods.

example

Assume that a firm has the following Balance Sheet at the end of a particular year.

Cash	10
Accounts Receivable	20
Inventory	15
Investment (Available for Sale)	5
Property, Plant & Equipment	50
Accumulated Depreciation	(10)
Total	**90**
Accounts Payable	15
Note Payable	20
Stock	40
Retained Earnings	15
Total	**90**

Assume that the firm had the following transactions over the course of the ensuing year.

We provide the journal entries for each transaction. We also label the cash flows in "real time," as before, followed by the alternative methods.

1. The firm bought inventory for $5 on credit.

Assets	Liabilities	Owners' Equity
5 Inventory	5 Account Payable	

2. The firm paid for the inventory purchased above.

Assets	Liabilities	Owners' Equity
(5) Cash (CFO)	(5) Account Payable	

3. The firm sold $5 of the inventory for $20 on account.

Assets	Liabilities	Owners' Equity
20 A/R		20 Revenue
(5) Inventory		(5) Cost of Goods Sold

4. The firm collected $18 from customers.

Assets	Liabilities	Owners' Equity
(18) A/R		
18 Cash (CFO)		

5. The firm bought Property, Plant & Equipment (PP&E) for $10 cash.

Assets	Liabilities	Owners' Equity
10 PP&E		
(10) Cash (CFI)		

6. The firm borrowed $2 from a bank.

Assets	Liabilities	Owners' Equity
2 Cash (CFF)	2 Note Payable	

7. The firm accrued wages of $4.

Assets	Liabilities	Owners' Equity
	4 Wages Payable	(4) SG&A Expense

8. The firm paid the above accrued wages.

Assets	Liabilities	Owners' Equity
(4) Cash (CFO)	(4) Wages Payable	

9. The firm depreciated PP&E by $4.

Assets	Liabilities	Owners' Equity
(4) Accumulated Depreciation		(4) Depreciation Expense

10. The firm accrued interest of $1.

Assets	Liabilities	Owners' Equity
	1 Interest Payable	(1) Interest Expense

11. The firm accrued taxes of $2.

Assets	Liabilities	Owners' Equity
	2 Tax Payable	(2) Tax Expense

12. The firm paid a dividend of $3 cash.

Assets	Liabilities	Owners' Equity
(3) Cash (CFF)		(3) Retained Earnings

13. The firm closed its books.

Assets	Liabilities	Owners' Equity
		(20) Revenue
		5 Cost of Goods Sold
		4 SG&A Expense
		4 Depreciation Expense
		1 Interest Expense
		2 Tax Expense
		4 Retained Earnings

EXHIBIT 7.1

Event Numbers	Cash	Accounts Receivable	Inventory	Investment	PP&E	Accumulated Depreciation	Total
Begin	10	20	15	5	50	(10)	**90**
1			5				
2	(5)						
3		20					
3			(5)				
4	18	(18)					
5	(10)				10		
6	2						
7							
8	(4)						
9						(4)	
10							
11							
12	(3)						
13							
End	8	22	15	5	60	(14)	**96**

	Accounts Payable	Wages Payable	Interest Payable	Tax Payable	Note Payable	Stock	Retained Earnings	Total
Begin	15	0	0	0	20	40	15	**90**
1	5							
2	(5)							
3								
3								
4								
5								
6					2			
7		4						
8		(4)						
9								
10			1					
11				2				
12						(3)		
13							4	
End	15	0	1	2	22	40	16	**96**

	Revenue	Cost of Goods Sold	SG&A Expense	Depreciation Expense	Interest Expense	Tax Expense
Begin	0	0	0	0	0	0
1						
2						
3	20					
3		(5)				
4						
5						
6						
7			(4)			
8						
9				(4)		
10					(1)	
11						(2)
12						
13	(20)	5	4	4	1	2
End	0	0	0	0	0	0

In **Exhibit 7.1**, we show the ledger and the Balance Sheet.

The Income Statement is provided below:

Revenue	20
Cost of Goods Sold	(5)
SG&A Expense	(4)
Depreciation Expense	(4)
Interest Expense	(1)
Tax Expense	(2)
Net Income	**4**

The cash account from the ledger is shown in **Exhibit 7.2**, along with the labels for the individual cash flows.

EXHIBIT 7.2

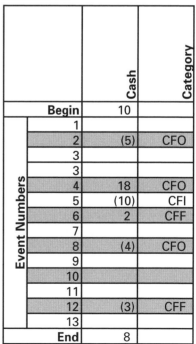

Event Numbers	Cash	Category
Begin	10	
1		
2	(5)	CFO
3		
3		
4	18	CFO
5	(10)	CFI
6	2	CFF
7		
8	(4)	CFO
9		
10		
11		
12	(3)	CFF
13		
End	8	

The total cash flows by category are provided below:

	Individual Cash Flows from the Cash Account	Total
Cash from Operating Activities (CFO)	- 5 + 18 - 4	9
Cash Used in Investing Activities (CFI)	-10	(10)
Cash Used in Financing Activities (CFF)	+ 2 - 3	(1)
Total Change in Cash		**(2)**
Beginning Cash Balance		10
Ending Cash Balance		8

We add more descriptions to our categories and produce the Statement of Cash Flows below:

Cash from Customers	18
Cash to Employees	(4)
Cash for Inventory	(5)
Total CFO	**9**
Cash for Purchase of PP&E	(10)
Total CFI	**(10)**
Cash from the Bank	2
Cash for Dividends	(3)
Total CFF	**(1)**
Total Change in Cash	**(2)**

The two alternative methods for deriving the Statement of Cash Flows are called the direct method and the indirect method.

In the ◀direct method▶, the individual cash flows are identified through transaction analysis. In transaction analysis, we re-create an account or a journal entry from data given in the Income Statement and Balance Sheets. We recreate the account or journal entry in order to help us identify relevant cash flows.

In the ◀indirect method▶, Net Income, which is accrual based, and therefore contains non-cash sales and expenses, is adjusted to remove these non-cash items. Almost all firms use the indirect method.

Direct Method

We will start with the direct method. Above, we labeled the cash flows in "real time." However, with the direct method, we recreate transactions after the fact and then label the cash flows in summary fashion. Firms could have thousands of credit sales and subsequent cash collections. Rather than labeling the cash collections individually, the direct method waits until the end of the accounting period and labels them as a group.

Transaction analysis recreates the changes in the accounts. We know the beginning and ending balances from the consecutive Balance Sheets. Additionally, we have the Income Statement.

For instance, Accounts Receivable increases with credit sales. Below is the Accounts Receivable account. Given the beginning and ending balances from the consecutive Balance Sheets, and given the effect of credit sales on Accounts Receivable, we simply have to solve for "x," the cash flow.

Accounts Receivable

Beginning Balance	+ / – Increases and Decreases	= Ending Balance
	+ Credit Sales – Cash Received from Credit Customers (CFO)	
20	20 – x	22

x=18 = Cash Received from Customers

We know this also from the journal entry 4 above. This simple example, with only one cash receipt from customers, does not reflect reality because firms have so many cash collections over a fiscal period. Transaction analysis would allow us to identify and label all these cash flows at the end of the period as a group. It is not practical to label cash flows in real time in real life.

Let's go around the Balance Sheet, one account at a time, and solve for the related cash flows. We will first consider the remaining CFO-related accounts, beginning with inventory. To see how much cash was paid for inventory, we have to look at two accounts, Inventory and Accounts Payable. We first solve for the amount of inventory purchased. Then, we solve for the payments in the Accounts Payable account.

Inventory

Beginning Balance	+/- Increases and Decreases	= Ending Balance
	+ Purchases – Cost of Goods Sold	
15	+ x – 5	15

x = 5 = Purchases

Here we solve for the amount of Inventory purchased, which is $5. We know this also from journal entry #1.

The cash flow associated with the purchase of inventory would be found in Accounts Payable.

Accounts Payable

Beginning Balance	+/- Increases and Decreases	= Ending Balance
	+ Purchases – Cash Payments (CFO)	
15	+ 5 – x	15

x = 5 = Cash Payments (CFO)

We also know the amount paid to suppliers from journal entry #2.

The next CFO-related account is Wages Payable.

Wages Payable

Beginning Balance	+/- Increases and Decreases	= Ending Balance
	+ Wage Expense (or SG&A) – Cash Payments (CFO)	
0	+ 4 – x	0

x = 4 = Cash Payments (CFO)

The firm must have paid the exact amount of accrued wages, since the beginning and ending balances are both zero. We can also see this from journal entries 7 and 8.

The only remaining CFO-related accounts are Interest Payable and Tax Payable. We are reminded that even though it makes more sense to classify cash paid for interest as CFF, it is classified under U.S. GAAP as CFO.

Interest Payable

Beginning Balance	+/- Increases and Decreases	= Ending Balance
	+ Interest Expense – Cash Payments (CFO)	
0	+ 1 – x	1

x = 0 = Cash Payments (CFO)

We can see in journal entry 10 that the firm accrued Interest Expense of $1, but did not subsequently pay it.

Finally, we perform transaction analysis on Tax Payable.

Tax Payable

Beginning Balance	+/- Increases and Decreases	= Ending Balance
	+ Tax Expense – Cash Payments (CFO)	
0	+ 2 – x	2

x = 0 = Cash Payments (CFO)

Similar to interest, we can see in journal entry 11 that the firm accrued Tax Expense, but did not subsequently pay it.

Next, we go to the CFI-related accounts and continue with the identical transaction analysis.

We start with the Available for Sale Investment.

Investment

Beginning Balance	+/- Increases and Decreases	= Ending Balance
	+ Purchases of Investments (CFI) – Sales of Investments (CFI)	
5	+ 0 – 0	5

We can see that there was no activity in the Investment account, and therefore no cash flows.

The next CFI-related account is PP&E. We will also recreate the contra-account, Accumulated Depreciation.

Property, Plant & Equipment

Beginning Balance	+/– Increases and Decreases	= Ending Balance
	+ Purchases of PP&E (CFI) – Sales of PP&E (CFI)	
50	+ 10 – 0	60

Thus, we see that the firm must have spent $10 on new PP&E and sold none. We see the purchase of PP&E in journal entry 5.

Accumulated Depreciation

Beginning Balance	+/– Increases and Decreases	= Ending Balance
	– Depreciation Expense + Sales of PP&E*	
–10	– 4 + 0	–14

As we saw in an earlier chapter, when PP&E is sold, the amount of Accumulated Depreciation that is associated with the sold portion is removed from the account. A "+" reduces the contra-account, because the account has a negative balance.

Finally we apply transaction analysis to the CFF-related accounts.

The first account is Note Payable.

Note Payable

Beginning Balance	+/– Increases and Decreases	= Ending Balance
	+ New Borrowings (CFF) – Repayments (CFF)	
20	+ 2 – 0	22

Thus, we see that the firm borrowed $2 of cash and did not make any repayments of principal. We see the new borrowing in journal entry 6.

The next CFF-related account is the Stock account.

Stock

Beginning Balance	+/– Increases and Decreases	= Ending Balance
	+ New Stock Issues (CFF)*	
40	0	40

*When Stock is repurchased, we would use the

Treasury Stock account, so we do not show a reduction in this account for repurchased shares. Therefore, we show only the increases in this account, of which there were none.

Finally, we analyze Retained Earnings.

Retained Earnings

Beginning Balance	+/– Increases and Decreases	= Ending Balance
	+ Net Income – Dividends (CFF)	
15	+ 4 – 3	16

Thus, we see that the firm paid $3 for dividends, which are classified as CFF. We see the dividend payment in journal entry 12.

We have concluded the transaction analysis of all accounts. Now we must simply organize the data, which we have done below.

Cash from Customers	18
Cash to Employees	(4)
Cash for Inventory	(5)
Total CFO	**9**
Cash for Purchase of PP&E	(10)
Total CFI	**(10)**
Cash from the Bank	2
Cash for Dividends	(3)
Total CFF	**(1)**
Total Change in Cash	**(2)**

As we see, the above Statement of Cash Flows is identical to the one we created when we labeled the cash flows in real time. Labeling cash flows in real time, in this example, seems much easier than using the direct method and having to do all of the transaction analysis. We agree. However, in reality, the number of cash transactions are too numerous to try to track in real time.

Admittedly, the direct method is quite laborious. The next method is used more often and is quite quick. What we gain in quickness and simplicity, however, we lose in intuition. The next method, the indirect method, is not as conceptually intuitive as the direct method, but it is easy.

Indirect Method

The indirect method pertains only to Cash from Operations (CFO). CFI and CFF would be calculated as before.

The indirect method begins with Net Income. We recall that Net Income is based upon the accrual accounting system. Therefore, Net Income will contain some non-cash items, such as non-cash revenues, and non-cash expenses. For instance in our example above, Interest Expense, Tax Expense, and Depreciation Expense were all non-cash expenses. We remember that the cash system of accounting recognizes only cash events. The indirect method converts Net Income to "Cash Income," or CFO, by removing all non-cash amounts.

The indirect method begins with Net Income and makes all of the necessary adjustments to remove non-cash items and to "strip away" excess accruals.

We provide explanations next to the adjustments below:

Net Income	4	We begin with Net Income and below we correct it for all of the items that do not involve cash.
+ Depreciation Expense	+ 4	Depreciation Expense reduces Net Income but it does not involve cash. Thus, we must **add** Depreciation Expense back to Net Income to compensate for the fact that it does not involve cash.
– Change in Accounts Receivable	-2	Net Income contains revenues of $20. However, only $18 of cash was collected. Therefore we have to subtract $2 from Net Income. Alternatively stated, the $2 **increase** in the A/R is subtracted. A/R **increased** by $2 because revenues from credit sales were $20, but cash collections were only $18.
+ Change in Interest Payable	+ 1	Net Income contains Interest Expense of $1 but no cash was paid. Interest Expense reduces Net Income, so we have to add $1 back to Net Income in order to compensate for the fact that the expense was non-cash. Alternatively stated, the $1 **increase** in Interest Payable is **added**.

+ Change in Tax Payable	+ 2	Similar to above, Tax Expense reduces Net Income, but Tax Expense was non-cash, so it must be added back to Net Income. Alternatively stated, the $2 **increase** in Tax Payable is **added**.
Total CFO	= 9	

Notice that CFO is the same ($9) using the Indirect Method, as it was when we labeled the cash flows in "real time," as well as when we used the direct method. Magic!

TRICKS OF THE TRADE

When analyzing a firm, the best place to find the firm's non-cash expenses, such as depreciation and amortization expense, is the Cash Flow Statement. Why not use the Income Statement? The Income Statement can have non-cash expenses in variety of locations such as Cost of Goods Sold and Selling, General and Administrative expenses. Unfortunately details for these locations might not always be available in the note disclosures. Plus, it is easier to look in one place – the Cash Flow Statement!

We can generalize the above procedure and create a formula to make the conversion from Net Income to CFO.

That formula is:

> **CFO = Net Income + Depreciation Expense**
> **– Changes in CFO-related Assets**
> **+ Changes in CFO-related Liabilities**

It is important to take note of the signs. The changes in CFO-related **Assets** are **subtracted**. The changes in CFO-related **Liabilities** are **added**. Specifically, if CFO-related Assets increase, then we subtract the change. If CFO-related Assets decrease, we add the change. If CFO-related Liabilities increase, we add the change. If CFO-related Liabilities decrease, we subtract the change. Just remember that Assets go in the "opposite direction," but Liabilities go in the "same direction" in making the conversion from Net Income to "Cash Income."

Stated alternatively, for all CFO-related Assets, we "flip" the signs. If the Asset increases, subtract the change. If the Asset decreases, add the change. For all CFO-related Liabilities, do not "flip" the signs. If the Liability increases, add the change. If the Liability decreases, subtract the change.

HINT

When thinking about the signs for Liabilities think about a loan from a bank to a firm. If the bank loans the firm more cash, the loan must increase on the firm's Balance Sheet (an increase in cash). Alternatively, if the firm pays back some of the loan to the bank in cash, the loan must decrease on the firm's Balance Sheet (a decrease in cash). The exact opposite happens for assets.

We provide several more examples below.

example
Indirect Method (without Dividends)

Assume a firm has the following Income Statement and comparative Balance Sheets:

Sales 120
Cost of Goods Sold.................................... (40)
Depreciation Expense................................ (10)
Interest Expense .... (10)
Income Before Tax...................................... 60

Income Tax Expense .... (24)
Net Income.. **36**

	Previous Year	Current Year	YOY Change
Cash	58	61	3
Accounts Receivable	32	50	18
Inventory	35	50	15
Investment	20	25	5
Property, Plant, & Equipment (PP&E)	130	150	20
Accumulated Depreciation	(50)	(60)	(10)
Total	**225**	**276**	**51**
Accounts Payable	30	38	8
Income Tax Payable	15	8	(7)
Notes Payable	100	120	20
Stock	40	40	0
Retained Earnings	40	76	36
Treasury Stock	0	(6)	(6)
Total	**225**	**276**	**51**

Below we repeat the formula for CFO using the Indirect Method:

CFO = Net Income + Depreciation − CFO-related Assets + CFO-related Liabilities

Inserting the numbers from the above Income Statement and comparative Balance Sheets, we have the following:

Cash from Operating Activities

Net Income.. 36
Depreciation Expense................................. 10
Increase in Accounts Receivable .... (18)
Increase in Inventory .... (15)
Increase in Accounts Payable 8
Decrease in Income Tax Payable.. (7)
Total Operating Cash Flow 14

Finishing with CFI and CFF

Now, let's extend the Cash Flow Statement to the remaining two categories, namely, CFI and CFF. For CFI, we inspect each CFI-related asset. We could reconstruct each account using transaction analysis, but we really do not need to do such an involved analysis. Rather, we can just inspect the account to see if a CFI-related asset increases. If so, we assume that cash was spent to acquire the asset. This would suggest a cash outflow. If the CFI-related asset decreases, we assume that an asset was sold, suggesting a cash inflow.

In our example, we have two CFI-related Assets: Investment and PP&E. The Investment increased by $5 and PP&E increased by $20. Therefore, we assume that the firm spent cash to acquire both assets. Therefore, CFI is negative $25.

Similarly, for CFF, we inspect each CFF-related Liability and Owners' Equity account. If a CFF-related Liability or Owners' Equity account increases, we assume that the firm received cash from a creditor or investor. If a CFF-related Liability or Owners' Equity account decreases, we assume that the firm paid cash to creditors or investors.

The Note Payable increased by $20, so we assume that the firm received cash from a bank. Treasury Stock increased by $6, so we assume that the firm bought back stock for $6. We are reminded that Treasury Stock is a contra-equity account, meaning that it has a negative balance.

We need to inspect Retained Earnings more closely, because it has two potential changes that are related to different cash flow categories. Net Income is CFO-related, but Dividends are CFF. Given Net Income, we calculate the amount of dividends.

Ending Retained Earnings

Beginning Retained Earnings	+ –	Net Income Dividends Paid	= Ending Balance Retained Earnings
40	+	36 – 0	76

Thus, we see that the firm did not pay a dividend, because the change in Retained Earnings is explained entirely by Net Income.

We now have our complete Statement of Cash Flows below:

Statement of Cash Flows	
Cash from Operating Activities	
Net Income	36
Depreciation Expense	10
Increase in Accounts Receivable	(18)
Increase in Inventory	(15)
Increase in Accounts Payable	8
Decrease in Income Tax Payable	(7)
Total Operating Cash Flows	14
Cash Used in Investing Activities	
Increase in Investments	(5)
Increase in PP&E	(20)
Total Investing Cash Flows	(25)
Cash from Financing Activities	
Increase in Note Payable	20
Repurchase of Common Stock	(6)
Total Financing Activities	14
Total Change in Cash	3
Beginning Cash Balance	58
Ending Cash Balance	61

example
Indirect Method (with Dividends)

Assume that the above firm paid a dividend. All of the steps in this example would be the same as above, which we do not repeat, except for the analysis of Retained Earnings.

Sales	120
Cost of Goods Sold	(40)
Depreciation Expense	(10)
Interest Expense	(10)
Income Before Tax	60
Income Tax Expense	(24)
Net Income	**36**

	Previous Year	Current Year	YOY Change
Cash	58	51	(7)
Accounts Receivable	32	50	18
Inventory	35	50	15
Investment	20	25	5
Property, Plant, & Equipment (PP&E)	130	150	20
Accumulated Depreciation	(50)	(60)	(10)
Total	**225**	**266**	**41**
Accounts Payable	30	38	8
Income Tax Payable	15	8	(7)
Notes Payable	100	120	20
Stock	40	40	0
Retained Earnings	40	66	26
Treasury Stock	0	(6)	(6)
Total	**225**	**266**	**41**

Notice that Retained Earnings changes by $26, but also notice that Net Income was $36. Thus, the firm must have paid dividends of $10. We have to split the $26 change in Retained Earnings into its CFO component ($36 Net Income) and its CFF component ($10 dividend).

Retained Earnings

Beginning Balance	+ –	Net Income Dividends Paid	= Ending Balance
40	+	36 – 10	66

The Cash Flow Statement is shown below. It is identical to the previous example, except for CFF. In the earlier example, CFF was $14. In this example, it is $4, because of the $10 dividend payment. Additionally, in the previous example, the ending cash balance was $61. In this example, it is $51, again due to the dividend payment. CFO and CFI are unaffected by the payment of the dividend.

101

Statement of Cash Flows	
Cash from Operating Activities	
Net Income	36
Depreciation Expense	10
Increase in Accounts Receivable	(18)
Increase in Inventory	(15)
Increase in Accounts Payable	8
Decrease in Income Tax Payable	(7)
Total Operating Cash Flows	14
Cash Used in Investing Activities	
Increase in Investments	(5)
Increase in PP&E	(20)
Total Investing Cash Flows	(25)
Cash from Financing Activities	
Increase in Note Payable	20
Repurchase of Common Stock	(6)
Dividends Paid	(10)
Total Financing Activities	4
Total Change in Cash	(7)
Beginning Cash Balance	58
Ending Cash Balance	51

	Previous Year	Current Year	YOY Change
Cash	58	63	5
Accounts Receivable	32	50	18
Inventory	35	50	15
Investment	20	16	(4)
Property, Plant, & Equipment (PP&E)	130	150	20
Accumulated Depreciation	(50)	(60)	(10)
Total	**225**	**269**	**44**
Accounts Payable	30	38	8
Income Tax Payable	15	8	(7)
Notes Payable	100	120	20
Stock	40	40	0
Retained Earnings	40	69	29
Treasury Stock	0	(6)	(6)
Total	**225**	**269**	**44**

example

Indirect Method (with Dividends and a Gain)

In the previous examples, the firm purchased an investment, resulting in a cash outflow of $5. The cash outflow was classified as CFI. In this example, the firm sold an investment, rather than purchased one, and the firm booked a gain of $5. The gain is reflected in the Income Statement below.

Sales 120
Cost of Goods Sold.. (40)
Depreciation Expense...................................... (10)
Interest Expense .... (10)
Gain.. 5
Income Before Tax.. 65
Income Tax Expense .... (26)
Net Income.. **39**

Whenever there is a gain or loss on the Income Statement, we need to perform transaction analysis and recreate the transaction that gave rise to the gain or loss. Since the investment decreases by $4 and the gain is $5, then the cash received must have been $9.

Below is the recreated transaction of the sale of the investment for a gain. We know the change in the Investment account and we know the gain, which will increase Owners' Equity. Thus, we solve for the amount of cash received.

Assets	Liabilities	Owners' Equity
(4) Investment 9 Cash = "x"		5 Gain

Earlier, we gave the following equation for calculating CFO using the indirect method:

CFO = Net Income + Depreciation – Change in CFO-related Assets + Change in CFO-related Liabilities

Now we must extend it to handle gains and losses. The extended equation is:

> **CFO = Net Income + Depreciation + Losses – Gains – Change in CFO-related Assets + Change in CFO-related Liabilities**

Gains are subtracted from Net Income, and losses are added back to Net Income. Neither gains nor losses pertain to CFO. By definition, gains and losses are from peripheral activities, not operating activities. Also, gains and losses do not correspond to the actual amount of cash received. In our example, the gain was $5, but the cash received was $9. For these reasons, we have to eliminate the gains and losses from Net Income.

TIPS OF THE TRADE

It may seem a bit strange to subtract gains and add losses to Net Income under the Indirect Method. We must treat these gains and losses this way so that the gain or loss is not counted twice in the Cash Flow Statement since the cash collected from this activity (which is not a central part of the firm's activities) is entirely classified as CFI. After all, the Cash Flow Statement must balance!

The firm also paid a dividend. We know this because Retained Earnings increases by $29, and Net Income is $39. Therefore, the dividend, as before, is $10.

The Cash Flow Statement is below.

We see that the gain is subtracted from Net Income. We also see that the sale of the investment is shown as CFI.

Statement of Cash Flows	
Cash from Operating Activities	
Net Income	39
Depreciation Expense	10
Gain	(5)
Increase in Accounts Receivable	(18)
Increase in Inventory	(15)
Increase in Accounts Payable	8
Decrease in Income Tax Payable	(7)
Total Operating Cash Flows	12

Cash Used in Investing Activities	
Sale of Investment	9
Increase in PP&E	(20)
Total Investing Cash Flows	(11)

Cash from Financing Activities	
Increase in Note Payable	20
Repurchase of Common Stock	(6)
Dividends Paid	(10)
Total Financing Activities	4

Total Change in Cash	5
Beginning Cash Balance	58
Ending Cash Balance	63

At this point in the text, we have covered many measurement and disclosure issues. Understanding how accounting events are measured and disclosed is useful for analyzing and interpreting Financial Statements, to which we now turn.

Chapter 8: Introduction to Basic Ratios and Analysis

BEFORE WE BEGIN

How do we go about analyzing a firm? It is helpful to keep in mind what the goal of the analysis is. The goal is almost always to make some decision about the firm, such as whether to lend to the firm, or to invest in the firm, or perhaps to sell to or buy from the firm. In order to make such decisions, we want to predict some relevant aspect of the firm's future. We want to know where the firm is going, more so than where it has been. Creditors want to predict a firm's ability to pay the interest and principal. Investors would like to predict the firm's ability to generate cash flows that can support payments of dividends, as well as new investments in growth opportunities, both of which will likely increase the value of the firm and therefore the stock price. Competitors, customers, and vendors study firms too. A competitor may wish to study the firm's strategy to know if a competitive threat will increase, impacting its own future. Customers and vendors may be interested in determining whether the firm would be able to service its products or pay its bills.

However, even though the focus is on a firm's future, analysis almost always begins with background information. Such background data will provide context, and context is important for making predictions.

We obviously need Financial Statements. We recommend obtaining the original statements filed with the government (such as the SEC in the United States) or the firm's Annual Report on the firm's website. Many sources of financial data (including those from subscription-based web sites) condense and summarize the Financial Statements, and they rarely include the note disclosures. Thus, from such data sources, it is not unusual to find, for example, listed among a firm's assets a category labeled "Other Assets" and this category can be the largest one. Without notes to explain what has been lumped into the category, potentially valuable information is lost. Moreover, financial databases sometimes have mistakes.

In addition to formal filings with the SEC, firms provide relevant and more timely information in web casts and press releases. Firm's websites usually have a link for investors.

> **TIPS OF THE TRADE**
>
> A firm will usually post its Financial Statements (such as an Annual Report) and other relevant information in the "investor relations" section of the firm's website. Sometimes the investor relations section is referred to as "for investors" and can be found within the "company information" or "about us" areas on the firm's home page.

The background information will allow us to analyze a firm's position in its industry. That analysis will be both quantitative and qualitative. Quantitative analysis would include the calculation and interpretation of relevant ratios which are benchmarked against a competitor and industry, as well as across time. Qualitative analysis may include an assessment of the firm's Strengths,

Weaknesses, Opportunities, and Threats, a so-called "SWOT" analysis. SWOT is useful because it combines both an assessment of the firm's current situation and forces us to assess what lies ahead in terms of opportunities and threats.

Next, we make a prediction about a likely outcome of interest. For example, investors want to predict the firm's future cash generating ability. The cash flows that investors try to predict are called "leveraged free cash flows," which they then discount using a relevant discount rate, called the "equity cost of capital." These discounted cash flows represent an estimate of the firm's value for stockholders and therefore help investors decide whether the firm is "fairly" valued. If the discounted value of leveraged free cash flows (that is, the estimate of the firm's fair value) is lower than the observed value (quoted stock price), then the investor may conclude that the firm is overvalued, in which case the investor would sell the stock, or at least not buy it. The techniques of firm valuation are covered in finance.

> Interested in how to value a firm? Check out Training The Street's self study "Fundamentals of Corporate Valuation" at **www.ttsuniversity.com**.

The process of analysis and prediction is filled with assumptions and estimates. Therefore, we would want to perform a sensitivity analysis. Sensitivity analysis includes changing several assumptions to see if we would still reach the same or similar conclusion about the firm's future.

In sum, the analytical framework is as follows:

1. *Choose a purpose for the analysis and relevant decision criteria.*
2. *Gather data.*
3. *Perform quantitative and qualitative assessments of data.*
4. *Predict the relevant future, based upon the above steps.*
5. *Conduct a sensitivity test on the prediction and make a decision.*

Before we analyze a real firm, we need some analytical tools to proceed. To that end, we will use a stylized example for pedagogical purposes, and focus on how to calculate a standard set of ratios.

RATIO WARNINGS

> **A BIT OF PERSPECTIVE**
>
> These ratio warnings are part of a discussion from Chapter 2. Financial Statement Analysis is an art that requires pulling together different pieces of information and putting that information to work.

Before we dive into ratios, a few words of caution are enumerated below:

1. *A ratio for the sake of a ratio is meaningless. We could pick any two numbers and create a ratio—say, the average outside temperature for the month of August and divide by the number of employees, and we would have degrees per employee. Is this useful?*

2. *Further, some ratios do not mean much in certain contexts. Inventory-related ratios are useless for firms with no inventory.*

3. *Ratios act as a proxy for constructs. Constructs are ideas. They cannot be seen or measured scientifically.*

   Leverage is a construct. We usually measure leverage with components from the Balance Sheet, such as total debt divided by total assets. What we hope to capture is an element of risk. Risk is an important element in an investment decision. Higher leverage ratios typically correspond to higher risk.

   Profitability is another construct. We usually use some Income Statement number, often scaled by a Balance Sheet number to try to capture some element of profitability as a measure of firm performance or success. An example might be Net Income divided by Total Assets, which is also called "Return on Assets." Performance is another important element in an investment decision.

4. *Ratios can badly mis-measure a construct. For example, a ratio can be distorted for reasons that do not reflect underlying economic reality. Consider Return on Equity (Net Income / Owners Equity). It is possible that both the numerator and the denominator are negative, reflecting a "sick" firm. However, the ratio would be positive,*

precisely because both the numerator and denominator are negative. Thus, we must be cautious and not mechanically calculate ratios without thinking about our results and whether we are measuring what we think we are measuring.

5. We must also benchmark ratios against the firm's past ratios and against the ratios of a competitor or industry average. Return on Equity (ROE) of 10% means little without a fuller context of what ROE is for the firm's competitors and what it was in previous periods.

6. Although it is true that ratios help investors understand the past, what most investors want to know is the future. By themselves, ratios are not particularly good predictors of the future. Combinations of ratios, along with textual disclosures from the firm's management, can help investors better predict a firm's future. Financial analysts spend a good deal of time trying to build a financial model, called a pro forma model, of the firm's future financial position and results. Building and studying past ratios may be a worthy exercise, but for most interested parties, only to the extent that it helps predict the future.

    There is one notable exception. Scrutiny of past ratios over time or against a competitor may signal that something is awry in the firm's accounting. In fact, regulators such as the SEC use such analysis as a screening technique for requesting additional information from firms. For example, the SEC would be "curious" to know why a firm is doing well while all others in the same industry are not.

7. The only standardized ratios are Basic and Diluted Earnings per Share. The FASB and IASB have very specific and highly technical rules for measuring these two ratios. Although there may be widespread agreement on how to construct many or most of the other commonly used ratios, there can still be wide variation.

Therefore, if ratios from third parties are used, such as from Bloomberg, Reuters, S&P, or Thomson, then it is a good idea to check how the ratios are constructed. If ratios from several data sources are used, an apples-to-apples comparison needs to be assured. Different organizations simply have different ways of measuring a similarly named ratio.

Let's now turn to our stylized example, beginning with a quick review of the accounting cycle. We will then calculate and discuss numerous ratios. The ratios presented are only representative; there are many more, but these are very common.

STYLIZED EXAMPLE OF THE ACCOUNTING CYCLE AND RATIOS

Assume the following balance sheet:

Cash 25
Accounts Receivable 20
Inventory 30
Property, Plant & Equipment............................. 130
Accumulated Depreciation....................................(50)
Total.. **155**

Accounts Payable 5
Notes Payable (Noncurrent) 100
Stock 10
Retained Earnings.. 40
Total.. **155**

Assume that the firm decided to do the following over the course of the year:

1. Buy $52 of inventory on account.

Assets	Liabilities	Owners' Equity
52 Inventory	52 Accounts Payable	

2. Sell for $90 on account inventory costing $60.

Assets	Liabilities	Owners' Equity
90 A/R		90 Revenue
(60) Inventory		(60) Cost of Goods Sold

3. Collect $80 of above sale.

Assets	Liabilities	Owners' Equity
80 Cash		
(80) A/R		

4. Pay $40 to suppliers of inventory.

Assets	Liabilities	Owners' Equity
(40) Cash	(40) A/P	

5. Buy Property, Plant & Equipment (PP&E) for $30 cash.

Assets	Liabilities	Owners' Equity
30 PP&E		
(30) Cash		

6. Incur and pay $6 of administrative expenses (SG&A).

Assets	Liabilities	Owners' Equity
(6) Cash		(6) SG&A Expense

7. Book $4 of depreciation expense.

Assets	Liabilities	Owners' Equity
(4) Accumulated Depreciation		(4) Depreciation Expense

8. Incur and pay $5 of interest expense.

Assets	Liabilities	Owners' Equity
(5) Cash		(5) Interest Expense

9. Book tax expense. The rate is 40%. There are no differences between the tax return and the accounting statement (Income Statement). The firm immediately paid cash of $6: (90-60-6-4-5)*40%

Assets	Liabilities	Owners' Equity
(6) Cash		(6) Tax Expense

10. Buy back $2 of stock.

Assets	Liabilities	Owners' Equity
(2) Cash)		(2) Treasury Stock

11. Pay a $3 cash dividend.

Assets	Liabilities	Owners' Equity
(3) Cash		(3) Retained Earnings

12. The firm closes its books.

Assets	Liabilities	Owners' Equity
		(90) Revenue
		60 Cost of Goods Sold
		6 SG&A Expense
		4 Depreciation Expense
		5 Interest Expense
		6 Tax Expense
		9 Retained Earnings

The above journal entries would then be posted to the ledger, as shown in **Exhibit 8.1**.

EXHIBIT 8.1

Event Numbers	Cash	Accounts Receivable	Inventory	PP&E	Accumulated Depreciation	Total	Accounts Payable	Notes Payable	Stock	Retained Earnings	Treasury Stock	Total	Revenue	Cost of Goods Sold	SG&A Expense	Depreciation Expense	Interest Expense	Tax Expense
Begin	25	20	30	130	(50)	**155**	5	100	10	40	0	**155**	0	0	0	0	0	0
1			52				52											
2		90											90					
2			(60)											(60)				
3	80	(80)																
4	(40)						(40)											
5	(30)			30														
6	(6)														(6)			
7					(4)											(4)		
8	(5)																(5)	
9	(6)																	(6)
10	(2)										(2)							
11	(3)									(3)								
12										9			(90)	60	6	4	5	6
End	13	30	22	160	(54)	**171**	17	100	10	46	(2)	**171**	0	0	0	0	0	**0**

We also derive the Cash Flow Statement below in the usual fashion:

CFO	
Net Income	9
Depreciation Expense	4
Increase in Accounts Receivable	(10)
Decrease in Inventory	8
Increase in Accounts Payable	12
Total	**23**

CFI	
Purchase of PP&E	(30)

CFF	
Repurchase of Stock	(2)
Dividends	(3)
Total CFF	**(5)**
Total Change in Cash	(12)
Beginning Cash Balance	25
Ending Cash Balance	13

On the next page, **Exhibit 8.2** shows the Income Statement and the consecutive Balance Sheets. We also provide our first set of ratios, Common Size (CS) ratios, and Year-over-Year (YOY) ratios.

EXHIBIT 8.2

	Previous Year	Current Year	YOY Change	Previous Year CS	Current Year CS
Cash	25	13	(0.48)	0.16	0.08
Accounts Receivable	20	30	0.50	0.13	0.18
Inventory	30	22	(0.27)	0.19	0.13
PP&E	130	160	0.23	0.84	0.94
Accumulated Depreciation	(50)	(54)	0.08	(0.32)	(0.32)
Total	**155**	**171**	**0.10**	**1.00**	**1.00**
Accounts Payable	5	17	2.40	0.03	0.10
Notes Payable (Noncurrent)	100	100	0.00	0.65	0.58
Stock	10	10	0.00	0.06	0.06
Retained Earnings	40	46	0.15	0.26	0.27
Trasury Stock	0	(2)	n/a	0.00	(0.01)
Total	**155**	**171**	**0.10**	**1.00**	**1.00**

Common size Financial Statements transform the raw Financial Statements into scaled or normalized statements in order to allow comparisons to other firms of different sizes or to the same firm at different points in time. Each item in the statement is converted to a percentage of a relevant total, such as Total Assets (for all Balance Sheet Items) and Sales (for the all Income Statement items).

This firm had 16% of Total Assets in cash in the previous year. The CS cash amount fell to 8% in current year. Such a decrease in the percentage of cash would probably need to be investigated. In a real situation, we would investigate by reading the firm's Management Discussion & Analysis (MD&A). The MD&A is a special section in the Annual Report or 10-K. In the MD&A, management must discuss the reasons for major changes in the Financial Statements.

In YOY terms, the cash balance fell 48% (from 25 to 13). Similar significant shifts occurred for most other asset categories, as well as Liabilities and Owners' Equity.

A fuller context would also be informative. Namely, we would want to compare the CS and YOY changes to the industry averages and to a comparable firm, which we do not have for this stylized example.

Below are listed numerous other ratios and their calculations. Next to each measure are brief commentaries.

We will also assume that this firm has 10 shares of stock outstanding and that the stock prices were $18 and $20 at sequential year ends. These data points are needed for "market-based" ratios.

As we illustrate each ratio, please refer to the underlying financial data, which is repeated in **Exhibit 8.3**:

EXHIBIT 8.3

Income Statement		Balance Sheet		
	Current Year		Previous Year	Current Year
Sales	90	Cash	25	13
Cost of Goods Sold	(60)	Accounts Receivable	20	30
SG&A Expense	(6)	Inventory	30	22
Depreciation Expense	(4)	PP&E	130	160
Interest Expense	(5)	Accumulated Depreciation	(50)	(54)
Income Before Tax	15	**Total**	**155**	**171**
Income Tax Expense	(6)	Accounts Payable	5	17
Net Income	9	Notes Payable (Noncurrent)	100	100
Dividends	3	Stock	10	10
		Retained Earnings	40	46
		Treasury Stock	0	(2)
		Total	**155**	**171**

1. ◄Profit Margin►

= Net Income / Sales

= 9 / 90

= 0.10

This is common-sized Net Income. It is sometimes called "Return on Sales." It is the "bottom line" (Net Income) divided by the "top line" (Sales) and shows how many cents of each dollar (or other currency) of sales made it all the way to the "bottom line" (10 cents, in this case).

Later we consider intervening margins, namely Gross Margin and EBIT Margin. All three margins are important. The Profit Margin is all inclusive and sometimes contains various gains and losses which can distort the results. Therefore, we need to consider the other margins which normally exclude these distortions.

2. ◄Asset Turnover►

= Sales / Average Total Assets

= 90/((.5)*(155+171))

= 0.552

Asset turnover shows how many dollars of sales are generated from each dollar of assets. It sheds light on how efficiently the assets are used to produce sales. In this case, each dollar of assets produces 55.2 cents of sales.

This ratio uses an Income Statement number (sales) and Balance Sheet numbers (total assets). Sometimes Income Statement numbers are called "flows" or "deltas." Balance Sheet numbers are balances or "sigmas" (sums). Therefore, since sales are a "delta" and total assets are a "sigma," analysts often average total assets, especially if total assets change significantly from the previous year. By averaging consecutive balance sheet numbers, a "flow" is approximated, which would match the flow implied by the income number. (Some people average, others simply do not. It is important to be consistent.)

By comparison to the above calculation, using the ending balance of assets, the Asset Turnover Ratio is:

= 90 / 171

= 0.526 (using ending balance)

We will not average the remaining ratios for purposes of simplicity.

3. ◄Leverage►

= Assets / Equity

= 171 / (10+46-2)

= 3.167

This shows how the firm is financed. For each dollar of equity, the firm has 3.167 dollars in assets, meaning that most assets are funded by debt. Thus, it is more debt financed than equity financed.

Leverage is also called the "equity multiplier" or the "debt burden ratio." However, we must note that there are many different ratios that are labeled "Leverage." This one uses Assets / Equity; others use Debt / Equity or Debt / (Debt + Equity), which is also called "debt to capital". Some of these other variations of "Leverage" are covered below.

4. ◄Return On Equity (ROE)►

= Net Income / Equity

= 9 / (10+46-2)

= 0.167

ROE relates the earnings of the firm to Owners' Equity, and it is a very popular performance measure. An underlying assumption is that the earnings of the firm belong to the firm's owners.

ROE is often calculated in the following alternative way, using the ratios 1-3 above.

ROE = **Profit Margin x Asset Turnover x Leverage**

= **Net Income / Sales x Sales / Assets x Assets / Equity**

= .10 x .526 x 3.167

= 0.167

Separating ROE into the three terms (Profit Margin, Asset Turnover, and Leverage) is known as the DuPont Method. It highlights, for instance, that a firm cannot simply increase sales to improve ROE (the sales cancel each other in the first 2 terms). Rather, a firm would have to increase the efficiency by which sales are generated.

Despite its popularity, there are severe limitations to ROE. First, it uses accounting measures in both the numerator and the denominator, and accounting measures can misrepresent economic reality. For example, the denominator is the book value of Owners' Equity, not its market value. Book value does not represent economic reality because it is based upon GAAP, and GAAP fails to capture the true economic picture of a firm for reasons we have seen. The numerator does not represent what the investor actually realizes as a return. Rather the numerator represents earnings, not cash, and the earnings of the firm are not literally paid to the firm's owners.

Second, sometimes ROE can "behave" in weird ways. For example, it is possible for Owners' Equity (the denominator) to be extremely small, due to, for example, a series of prior losses (which would have reduced Retained Earnings). If Owners' Equity is small, ROE could be inflated, leading to the false conclusion that the firm is doing particularly well.

Also, as mentioned before, a more embarrassing false conclusion could be drawn in the case of negative Net Income and negative Owners' Equity. This could be evidence of a very sick company, but the ratio would indicate a positive ROE (negative numerator divided by a negative denominator). Thus, some analysts avoid ROE and use some other measures, including ROA, described next.

5. ◄Return on Assets (ROA)►
= Net Income / Assets
= 9 / 171
= 0.053

ROA relates Net Income to the asset base, rather than to Owners' Equity, as above. ROA can also be calculated as the product of the first two terms of the DuPont Method, as below:

ROA = Profit Margin x Asset Turnover
= .10 x .526
= 0.053

Although ROA is arguably an improvement over ROE, it is only a marginal improvement, since it still uses Net Income in the numerator. (At least the denominator cannot be negative, as is the case with ROE.) Net Income can include items over which management has little or no control, such as various gains. The next measure is considered an improvement over Net Income.

6. ◄Earnings Before Interest and Taxes (EBIT)►
= Operating Earnings = Sales – Cost of Goods Sold – Selling, General and Administrative Expenses – R&D Expense – Depreciation and Amortization
= 90 - 60 - 6 - 4
= 20

Given the shortcomings of ROE and ROA (because of their use of Net Income), other performance measures incorporate EBIT, Earnings Before Interest and Taxes. EBIT focuses on core components of Net Income, whereas Net Income can include non-core items, such as various gains and losses. We will use EBIT in an upcoming ratio. First however, we address another measure that is closely related to EBIT.

> **A WORD ON TERMINOLOGY**
>
> Operating Earnings is also commonly referred to as a firm's Operating Profit.

7. ◄Earnings Before Interest Taxes Depreciatoin and Amortization (EBITDA)►
= EBIT + DA
= 20 + 4
= 24

Closely related to EBIT is EBITDA. EBITDA is often used as a crude proxy for Cash Flows from Operations (CFO), primarily because it is so easy to calculate. CFO is an important measure that is used in estimating a firm's value. (Valuation is covered in another course.) However, some feel that the calculation of CFO is laborious (although it really is not), so they have opted to use EBITDA as a surrogate. A problem with this surrogate is that it fails to adjust for changes in working capital (increases in inventory, for example), and it does not include the effects of interest and taxes, which are included in CFO. Thus, it is indeed a very rough proxy but used nonetheless.

To obtain depreciation and amortization, one must usually refer to the Statement of Cash Flows, since depreciation and amortization are sometimes not displayed as a "line item" in the Income Statement. That is, frequently firms will include depreciation and amortization as part of SG&A Expense. Also, most manufacturing firms must include some depreciation as part of Inventory and Cost of Goods

Sold. This is because under GAAP, inventory must include depreciation on physical assets used in the manufacturing process. However, the full amount of depreciation and amortization can be found in the Statement of Cash Flows.

So, where are we going with EBIT and EBITDA in terms of trying to find a better performance measure (over ROE and ROA)? EBIT is incorporated into a measure called Return on Invested Capital (ROIC). This measure receives a great deal of attention and represents another refinement.

However, before calculating ROIC, we need to calculate the "effective tax rate," "NOPAT," and "Market Cap," all three of which are used in ROIC.

8. ◄Effective Tax Rate►
= Income Tax Expense / Pretax Income
= 6 / 15
= 0.400

The effective tax rate is used in several upcoming ratios. As discussed earlier, the effective tax rate should not be confused with the statutory tax rate. The ◄statutory tax rate► is the rate passed by the various government bodies. In the U.S., Congress sets the statutory tax rates and the President signs the legislation that makes the rates official. Currently in the U.S., the statutory tax rate is 35%. However, firms' effective tax rates will typically differ from statutory tax rates, and we need to use the effective tax rate. Sometimes the effective tax rate is higher than the statutory tax rate, sometimes lower.

In this case, the assumed statutory tax rate is 40%, which also equals the firm's effective tax rate. This means that there are no permanent differences between GAAP income and taxable income. We covered an example of an item that can affect the effective tax rate in chapter 2. We saw that municipal interest reduced the effective tax rate because it is non-taxable income.

ROIC, which is where we are headed, uses EBIT after taxes (using the effective tax rate). Thus, we really need Earnings Before Interest but After Taxes. This is cumbersome to say. Some people just say "after tax EBIT." More commonly, this is called "Net Operating Profit after Taxes," or ◄NOPAT►.

9. ◄Net Operating Profit After Tax (NOPAT)►
= Net Operating Profit after Tax
= EBIT x (1-Effective Tax Rate)
= 20 x (1 - 0.40)
= 12

To obtain an after-tax amount of any tax related item one must multiply the pretax amount by 1-Effective Tax Rate, as shown below:

After Tax = Pretax – Taxes
= Pretax – Pretax x Effective Tax Rate
= Pretax x (1-Effective Tax Rate)

One more measure before calculating ROIC is Market Capitalization.

10. ◄Market Capitalization►
= Price per share x Number of shares outstanding

We are assuming that this firm has 10 shares outstanding, each currently worth $20.

= 20 x 10
= 200

Market Cap (as it is usually called) shows the value of a firm's equity at any given point in time.

Finally, we are ready to calculate ROIC.

11. ◄Return on Invested Capital (ROIC)►
= NOPAT / (Short-term debt obligations + Long Term Debt + Market Cap)
= 12 / (100 + 200)
= 0.040

ROIC is an improvement over ROE and ROA, because in the numerator, the focus is on a measure that is closer to cash flow (since most gains and losses are omitted) and since it represents the core earnings of the firm. Furthermore, the denominator focuses on the two main suppliers of financial capital: debt holders, as measured by interest bearing debt; and equity holders, as measured by Owners' Equity (at market values).

Most analysts suggest that all invested capital should be measured at market value, rather than book value, although sometimes book values are used for both. Here, we have used only the market value of equity. To calculate the market values of debt obligations, we need to look at quoted prices of the debt, which we will not do in this text.

In conclusion, although ROA is an improvement on ROE, and although ROIC is an improvement on ROA, ROIC still uses accounting-based measures in the numerator. Moreover, NOPAT does not represent "cash in hand" to investors. Therefore, one of the most relevant measures for shareholders is "Total Returns to Shareholders" (TRS).

12. ◄Total Return to Shareholders (TRS)►

= (Price per share$_t$ – Price per share$_{t-1}$ + Dividends per share$_t$) / Price per share$_{t-1}$

As previously mentioned, we are assuming that the current price per share is $20, the previous price per share was $18, and 10 shares are outstanding. We also remind ourselves that the firm paid a $3 dividend.

= (20 - 18 + 3/10) / 18
= 0.128

This shows how the firm has performed in the recent past (1 year) for its shareholders in terms of increasing the value of their investment. This change in wealth, however, is unrealized, unless the shareholder sells the share. Nonetheless, it is considered a measure of how much "better off," or "worse off," a stockholder is after having invested his or her money in the firm. The shareholders in this firm had TRS of 12.8%.

One caveat about TRS is that it captures historical changes in wealth. Although quite relevant, prior changes in stock prices are notoriously bad predictors of future changes. Some of the other measures (ROIC, ROA, etc.) are used in conjunction with TRS because these other (accounting-based) measures are shown to be associated with *future* changes in stock prices. Indeed a full analysis of a firm's performance requires a study of multiple ratios and "drilling" under these ratios to "sub-ratios" to try to uncover economic reality for the purposes of predicting a firm's likely future.

In fact, we will now drill down beneath some of the above measures. We will begin with the first component of the DuPont Method, which is Profit Margin (Net Income / Sales). This accounting-based measure of performance can be broken down into the cost ratio (COGS / Sales), SG&A ratio (SG&A Expense / Sales), etc. These ratios are the common size ratios and capture sub-components of Net Income (COGS, SG&A, etc.). These ratios were mentioned before but repeated here for completeness and ease of presentation.

13. ◄Cost Ratio►

= Cost of Goods Sold (COGS) / Sales
= 60 / 90
= 0.667

The cost ratio shows how much of sales are consumed by the cost of the product sold. If the cost ratio increases over time, this means that the firm is paying more for its inventory and is unable to pass along the cost increases in its selling prices, or that the firm had to cut its selling price to be able to sell slow moving inventory that it had already purchased.

14. ◄Gross Margin►

= (Sales – COGS) / Sales = 1- Cost Ratio
= (90-60)/90
= 0.333

The Cost Ratio and the Gross Margin sum to a value of 1.

Gross Margin is closely watched for just about any firm with significant levels of inventory, such as retailers. It shows the relation between selling prices and cost of product sold. During periods of inflation, when cost increases cannot be passed along to customers, we say that margins are being "squeezed" or that there is margin contraction. The opposite situation is referred to as margin expansion. For example, if the firm is able to increase selling prices while holding COGS flat, then margins expand. Margin expansion is a good sign; margin contraction is typically not.

A WORD ON TERMINOLOGY

Sales minus COGS is also referred to as a firm's Gross Profit.

---

15. ◄SG&A Ratio►

= SG&A Expense / Sales
= 6 / 90
= 0.067

The SG&A Ratio shows how much of sales are consumed by the Selling, General, and Administrative functions. If the SG&A Ratio changes over time, this means that the firm is unable to change SG&A Expenses exactly in sync with sales. Thus, whereas SG&A is usually considered a variable cost (meaning that it varies directly with sales), it is not perfectly correlated. A large portion of SG&A is often salary. Sometimes firms are not able to (or choose not to) hire (and fire) personnel exactly in accordance with sales increases and decreases. Like the Cost Ratio, the SG&A Ratio is a common size ratio.

16. ◄R&D Ratio►

= R&D Expense / Sales

= 0 / 90

= 0

The R&D Ratio shows how much of sales are consumed by the research and development function.

When a functional area is "immaterial," firms will typically not show it as a line item, but they will instead combine it with another functional area, such as SG&A, and often give details in the note disclosures. This is often the case with firms that have R&D but for whom it is not a material amount. However, for so-called intellectual property type firms (such as software firms or pharmaceuticals), R&D would be a significant amount and broken out as a line item on the Income Statement. In this example, we assume the firm had no R&D or that it is included with SG&A.

17. ◄EBIT Margin►

= EBIT / Sales

= 20 / 90

= 0.22

As previously mentioned, EBIT Margin is one of three main margins, which are Gross Margin, EBIT Margin, and Profit Margin. They are sequential margins, with Gross Margin at the top of the Income Statement (with only Cost of Goods Sold subtracted from sales), followed by EBIT Margin (with Cost of Goods Sold, SG&A Expense, R&D Expense, and Depreciation Expense subtracted from sales), followed by Profit Margin (with all expenses subtracted from sales). These check points allow us to find where inefficiencies are located. For

example, if Gross Margin improves but EBIT Margin deteriorates, then we know to check SG&A Expense, R&D Expense, or Depreciation Expense.

Staying with the DuPont Method, we now turn to the second term, the Asset Turnover Ratio (Sales / Total Assets), and drill beneath this ratio to analyze sub-turnovers.

···· ASK THE ACCOUNTING GURU ····

If someone were to ask you "how profitable is the firm" where would you look? A good place to start your analysis would be to examine the firm's Gross, EBIT and Profit Margins. From there, a thoughtful analysis might include the margins' trends and how these trends compare to the firm's peers.

18. ◄Accounts Receivable Turnover►

= Sales / Account Receivable

= 90 / 30

= 3.0

This measures the number of times over a fiscal period (in this case one year) that a firm collects its Accounts Receivable. The higher the number, the faster the cash is realized from credit sales. This firm collects its Accounts Receivable 3 times per year. This is one of those ratios that may require averaging the denominator, since the ratio includes both an Income Statement measure and a Balance Sheet measure. (Also, in our example, Accounts Receivable changes YOY by 50%, from $20 to $30. A change of this magnitude generally warrants averaging.) However, as previously stated, we will continue with the end-of-period number, rather than an average number.

19. ◄Inventory Turnover►

= Cost of Goods Sold / Inventory

= 60 / 22

= 2.7

This measures the number of times over a fiscal period (in this case one year) that a firm sells its inventory. The higher the number, the faster the firm is able to sell its inventory.

Just being able to sell inventory quickly is not by itself laudable. Some firms' strategies are focused more on margins than inventory turns. For example, a premium jeweler will have high margins but low inventory turns. A discount retailer would have low margins and high inventory turns.

The above turnovers (Accounts Receivable Turnover and Inventory Turnover) tell us approximately how many times in a year the firm collected its receivables and sold its inventory. However, variations of the above turnovers are often used, namely Days to Collect Receivables and Days to Sell Inventory. These two ratios simply convert the turnovers from "number of times" to "number of days."

"Days to collect receivables" is also often called Days Sales Outstanding (DSO) and "days to sell inventory" is often called Days Sales in Inventory (DSI).

20. ◀Days Sales Outstanding (DSO)▶

= 365 / Accounts Receivable Turnover

= 365 / 3

= 121.7

This converts Accounts Receivable Turnover into a measure based upon "days." (We use 365 days in the fiscal period to be consistent with our calculation of Accounts Receivable Turnover.) Thus, this firm collects its receivables in just under 122 days, on average. This appears to be a lengthy period of time between the sale and the collection of cash. The usual terms of a credit sale are about 30 days. However, in some industries, longer terms are in fact granted. When the payment is delayed for an extended period, the seller will often charge interest. We assume no interest in our simple example.

As with other ratios, we would want to see if and how this ratio changes over time, and we may become concerned to see it extend significantly. A significant increase in the number of days to get paid could mean that the firm changed its payment terms to allow customers to pay later than previously, or that the firm had sold to customers who had encountered financial difficulty and were unable to pay on time.

21. ◀Days Sales in Inventory (DSI)▶

= 365 / Inventory Turnover

= 365 / 2.727

= 133.8

This converts the Inventory Turnover into a measure based upon days. (We use 365 days in the fiscal period to be consistent with our calculation of Inventory Turnover). Thus, it takes approximately 134 days for the firm to sell its inventory, on average. This ratio varies considerably across industries. Valuable jewelry will take over a year or more to sell, on average. Food inventory (perishables) sells in a few days.

If this ratio were to increase, we may be concerned that the inventory is not moving as quickly as previously because the demand is no longer as strong. The change in demand could be related to macroeconomic variables or it could be related to firm specific variables. The latter could include issues with the quality of the product that the firm produces or with changes in consumer behavior.

22. ◀Operating Cycle▶

= DSO + DSI

= 121.7 + 133.8

= 255.5

The above two ratios (DSO and DSI) together constitute the operating cycle. The operating cycle approximates how long a firm must go before it gets the cash back from the investment in inventory. Cash goes out of the firm into inventory and does not come back to the firm until the customer pays. Long operating cycles often create the need for short term borrowings. One way to offset the Operating Cycle is to buy the inventory on credit and therefore not have to pay the supplier immediately.

Thus, we add one more term to the Operating Cycle, namely ◀Days Payable Outstanding (DPO)▶. This measures the average number of days that it takes for the firm to pay its suppliers for inventory. To calculate DPO, we must first calculate purchases.

23. ◀Purchases▶

= Ending Inventory + Cost of Goods Sold – Beginning Inventory

= 22 + 60 - 30

= 52

This can be seen from the journal entry earlier (journal entry 1), but we can also calculate the amount from the above equation.

Now we can calculate Accounts Payable Turnover.

24. ◄Accounts Payable Turnover►
= Purchases / Accounts Payable
= 52 / 17
= 3.1

This firm pays its vendors just over 3 times over a fiscal period (in this case one year).

TRICKS OF THE TRADE

Accounts payable turnover is often calculated as Cost of Goods Sold / Accounts Payable. Be careful when calculating, using and interpreting ratios as the inputs can vary significantly. The most important consideration is to be consistent in your approach.

---

25. ◄Days Payable Outstanding (DPO)►
= 365 / Accounts Payable Turnover
= 365/3.059
= 119.3

This converts the Accounts Payable Turnover into a measure based upon days. (We use 365 days in the fiscal period to be consistent with our calculation of Accounts Payable Turnover.) Thus, this firm pays its suppliers in about 119 days, on average. A significant reduction in DPO would be worrisome, since it may mean that the firm's suppliers are worried about extended payment terms and may be shortening the time to pay. In extreme cases, the terms become "cash only." That is, the suppliers will not sell to the firm on credit.

26. ◄Cash Cycle (or Days other Financing Required)►
= Operating Cycle - DPO
= 255.5 - 119.3
= 136.2

If we subtract DPO from the Operating Cycle, we obtain the "Cash Cycle." The Cash Cycle is also called "Days Other Financing Required."

The Cash Cycle can highlight short term liquidity needs. The Operating Cycle shows how long it takes the firm to receive the cash that it "invested" in the inventory and the receivable. DPO shows the days before payment is made to suppliers of inventory. Thus, a net positive result for the Cash Cycle must be funded through existing cash balances or short term loans.

Returning to the DuPont Method, we have looked at several measures thus far under the first two terms: Profit Margin and Asset Turnover. These two terms tell us how efficient the firm has been in controlling expenses and how efficiently it has employed assets to generate income and cash flows. The third term ("Leverage") focuses on the financing decision, and how much liquidity the firm maintains to finance its operations. We can drill underneath Leverage to measure sub-ratios, beginning with the Current Ratio.

27. ◄Current Ratio►
= Current Assets / Current Liabilities
= (13 + 30 + 22) / 17
= 3.824

The current ratio is a liquidity measure. Current Assets include cash and items that are expected to be used or consumed or turned into cash within one year. Current Liabilities are liquidated (paid) by Current Assets. Thus, Current Liabilities are essentially paid within one year, so this ratio shows how easily the firm will be able to cover its short term obligations.

Lenders (banks and suppliers who grant credit) prefer a high current ratio for comfort (somewhat in excess of 1). However, low current ratios do not necessarily mean trouble. For instance, a firm may have large gross margins, a solid credit rating, and unused lines of credit, all of which mitigate concerns over low current ratios.

A BIT OF PERSPECTIVE

The definition of a "good" ratio varies from firm to firm, industry to industry and with the ups and downs of the economy. For example, a current ratio of 1.4 could have been considered "good" for a residential construction firm in 2007. However in 2010, a current ratio of 1.1 might be considered "good" for the same firm given the residential construction industry's financial difficulty.

---

28. ◄Quick Ratio►

= Liquid Current Assets (mainly cash, marketable securities and receivables) / Current Liabilities

= (13 + 30) / 17

= 2.5

The Quick Ratio is a variation of the Current Ratio.

Included in Current Assets are some items that are less liquid (further from cash). For instance, inventory is an example. Work-in-process (WIP) inventory for a manufacturer is even less liquid, because WIP must be completed before it is ready for sale.

Therefore, rather than the Current Ratio, some prefer to use the Quick Ratio, because it excludes inventory and other less liquid items.

29. ◄Total Debt to Capital►

= (Short and Long Term Debt) / (Short and Long Term Debt + Owners' Equity)

= 100 / (100 + 10 + 46 - 2)

= 0.649

This shows how the firm is financed. It is another ratio that measures leverage, similar to ratio 3. Higher amounts correspond to higher funding by debt, relative to equity. Firms try to balance the costs and benefits of debt versus equity financing in their capital structure.

30. ◄Interest Coverage►

= EBIT / Interest Expense

= 20 / 5

= 4

The Interest Coverage Ratio shows the number of times that EBIT exceeds interest expense. It is one measure of the firm's ability to pay interest to creditors. Firms with higher ratios are considered to possess a greater ability to meet interest payments. Another variation of this ratio is calculated as EBITDA / Interest Expense.

A problem with the Interest Coverage Ratio is that interest payments require cash, not EBIT (or "earnings"). Thus, although the Interest Coverage Ratio is quite popular, EBIT includes many non-cash items, and creditors must be paid in cash. Thus, a better measure is one that uses Cash Flow from Operations (CFO) which we discuss next.

31. ◄Cash Interest Coverage►

= (CFO + cash payments for interest and income taxes) / cash payments for interest

= (23 + 5 + 6) / 5

= 6.800

As a reminder, in our stylized example, the firm had $23 of CFO and paid interest and taxes of $5 and $6, respectively.

32. ◄Effective Interest Rate (Pre-tax)►

= Interest Expense / Total Interest Bearing Debt

= 5 / 100

= 0.050

The effective interest rate represents a rough estimate of a firm's cost of debt financing. It is an estimate of the average rate that creditors are charging the firm on its debt. Riskier firms will have to pay a higher interest rate on their debt. There are other, more refined ways to measure the effective interest rate (such as calculating a yield-to-maturity, or estimating a synthetic yield). These alternative measures are covered in finance. For our purposes, we will simply use the specification above. However, we must adjust our above measure for the effect of taxes, which we do below.

33. ◄After Tax Effective Interest Rate►

= Effective Interest Rate (Pre-tax) x (1 - Effective Tax Rate)

= 5 x (1-.4) / 100

= 0.030

The Effective Interest Rate is typically calculated on an "after tax" basis since interest is usually deductible. Debt financing is in essence subsidized by the government because firms receive a tax deduction for interest.

34. ‹Dividend Payout Ratio›

= Total Dividends / Net Income

Or, on a per share basis:

Dividend Payout Ratio = Dividends per Share / Basic Earnings per Share

Using the former specification (not on a per share basis), we would calculate it as follows:

= 3 / 9

= 0.333

The firm paid one-third of its Net Income ("earnings") as a dividend.

Some firms are known as "dividend paying firms" which generally means that they have a long track record of paying a significant dividend. These firms are often called "income" investments, because they pay investors regular income in the form of a dividend. For example, utility firms often pay two-thirds or more of their earnings as a dividend. By contrast, high growth firms (sometimes called "growth" investments) may not pay a dividend at all because they need to retain the cash to invest in the numerous opportunities they have before them. Indeed there is wide variation across firms and industries in dividend policy.

Often firms state their dividend policy in terms of a percentage of earnings that they wish to pay out on an ongoing basis. However, they generally speak of average payouts over a period of time because earnings can fluctuate from year to year, and firms do not want their dividends to fluctuate as much as earnings. To do so would be to increase and decrease dividends as earnings go up and down.

Dividend policy is rather "sticky," meaning that firms do not deviate too much from prior year dividend amounts. A significant, unexpected reduction in dividends is usually interpreted negatively by the market. Investors fear that if the firm reduces its dividend, it is signaling that it does not expect to be able to generate the future cash flows to sustain the dividend. If firms increase the dividend, it is interpreted in the opposite way, namely that the firm will be able to generate adequate cash flows for sustaining the dividend at the higher level.

35. ‹Dividend Yield›

= Dividend per Share / Price per Share (using the fiscal year-end price per share).

= .3 / 20

= 0.015

The dividend yield is related to the dividend payout ratio. However, the dividend yield divides the dividend by the stock's price (rather than by the firm's earnings, as is the case with the payout ratio). If one were to buy this stock at the price of $20, it would yield only a 1.5% return. Thus, investors would be looking for stock price appreciation in addition to any dividend yield.

Conclusion

With this we have concluded our introductory work. We have covered a significant amount of:

- **vocabulary**: such as, capitalize, expense, accrue, defer, revenues, gains, losses, and expenses

- **methodology**: journalizing, posting, generating Financial Statements, deriving CFO both with direct and indirect methods, and calculating present value

- **interpretation**: calculating and interpreting ratios, understanding the shortcomings of accrual based accounting, and understanding the reasons for unbooked assets such as human capital and unbooked liabilities such as off-balance sheet leases

- **accounting measurement and disclosure issues**: deferred taxes, capitalized interest, capitalized depreciation, cost principle, revenue principle, matching principle, classified Financial Statements, impairments, restructurings, bond issues, lease accounting, stock issues and repurchases, Basic and Diluted EPS

- **theory**: agency theory, debt versus equity financing, life cycle of the firm, and information needs of investors and lenders

Throughout this text, we have kept it tractable by using only stylized examples. The real world can be a bit messy, in fact very messy at times. However, we need to go there to apply our skills because that's where the work is, and, actually, that is where the fun is, too. **The companion text to this Handbook will walk us through the analysis of a real company, using original filings at the SEC**.

We also conclude by underscoring the importance of understanding why we even want to study "real" firms. Generally, the reason deals with predicting "something," such as earnings, cash flows, growth, liquidity, etc. Thus, included in the companion book is a preview of how to go about setting up financial models that forecast these and other variables of interest. Although we stop short of actually building financial models in the accounting portion of our study, we lay the groundwork and assemble much of the necessary data from the Financial Statements. Finding relevant data buried in Financial Statements and the accompanying notes takes a bit of practice. We show you how to go about it in a fairly efficient way.

Information about the complete version of the Handbook that you just finished can be found at: *TheAccountingOasis.com*

If you have comments or questions about this text, please let me know. Thank you, and all the best.

Stephen Bryan, Ph.D.
30 Stevens Lane
Walpole, NH 03608
Stephen.Bryan@TheAccountingOasis.com

Glossary

Accelerated Method

Accelerated Methods are depreciation methods that recognize more Depreciation Expense early in an asset's life and less depreciation later in the asset's life. An Accelerated Method of depreciation contrasts with straight-line depreciation which is a constant amount of Depreciation Expense over the life of the asset. Double-declining Balance is an example of an Accelerated Method of depreciation.

Accounting Cycle

The Accounting Cycle is the process of 1) identifying all accounting events that must be recognized or disclosed, 2) valuing these events if possible, 3) recording the events, either via a journal entry or a note disclosure, 4) disclosing the events in Financial Statements, either as statement disclosures or note disclosures.

Accounts Payable Turnover

Accounts Payable Turnover = Purchases / Accounts Payable. Sometimes, rather than Purchases, Cost of Goods Sold is used in the numerator. When Accounts Payable changes significantly over a period, Average Accounts Payable is used in the denominator.

Accounts Receivable

Accounts Receivable are amounts a firm is owed from customers from previous credit sales. Accounts Receivable will generally be shown "net" of the Allowance for Doubtful Accounts. The difference between Accounts Receivable and the Allowance for Doubtful Accounts is referred to as the Net Realizable Value of the Accounts Receivable.

Accounts Receivable Turnover

Accounts Receivable Turnover = Sales / Accounts Receivable. When Accounts Receivable changes significantly over a period, Average Accounts Receivable is used in the denominator.

Accrual Accounting

Accrual accounting is the accounting system that recognizes revenue when it is earned (and realized or realizable) and that recognizes expenses when they are incurred. Thus, under the accrual accounting system, Revenues and Expenses can be recognized before, after, or simultaneously with the recognition of cash flows. It is a more complicated system than the cash system, and it requires some judgment to apply.

Accumulated Other Comprehensive Income (AOCI)

Accumulated Other Comprehensive Income (AOCI) is an Owners' Equity account that contains certain types of Gains and Losses. For instance, unrealized Gains and Losses under fair value accounting for Available for Sale Securities are recognized as AOCI, rather than as a Gains and Losses in the current Income Statement.

Additional Paid in Capital (APIC)

Additional Paid in Capital (APIC) represents the amount of investment from investors that is above the par value of a firm's common stock.

After Tax Effective Interest Rate

After Tax Effective Interest Rate = Effective Interest Rate (Pretax) x (1 - Effective Tax Rate)

Allowance for Doubtful Accounts

Allowance for Doubtful Accounts is a Contra-Account to Accounts Receivable. The balance of the Allowance for Doubtful Accounts is an estimate of the amount of the receivable that the firm does expect to collect from customers.

Amortizing Loan

An Amortizing Loan is a loan where the Principal is being reduced over time since the borrower's cash payments to the lender to pay back the loan are greater than the periodic Interest Expense.

Annuities

Annuities are a series of cash payments. Each cash payment is the same amount and occurs at a regular interval of time. In MicroSoft Excel, the annuity is denoted as "pmt" in the time value of money functions.

Asset Turnover

Asset Turnover = Sales / Total Assets

Available for Sale Securities

Available for Sale Securities are investments in securities that a firm purchases that are not classified as Trading Securities. Thus, Available-for-Sale Securities are typically expected to be held by the investor for a longer period of time, although the period of time is not specified. Available for Sale Securities are reported in the Balance Sheet as Current Assets or Non-current Assets, depending on when the firm anticipates selling them. Available for Sale Securities are carried at fair value. Contrary to Trading Securities, when the values of Available for Sale Securities change, the firm recognizes unrealized Gains and Losses as a component of the Balance Sheet (rather than the Income Statement), namely as Accumulated Other Comprehensive Income.

Average Cost Method

The Average Cost Method is a method for assigning costs of Inventory purchased or manufactured to inventory that is sold. The average costs of Inventory items purchased or produced are assigned to Cost of Goods Sold. If the first item in inventory cost $10 and the second cost $14, then, for the sale of a single item, Cost of Goods Sold is $12.

.... **B** ....

Balance Sheet

The Balance Sheet is one of the primary Financial Statements (besides the Income Statement and the Statement of Cash Flows). The Balance Sheet shows account balances at a point in time. The Balance Sheet, in equation form, is:
Assets = Liabilities + Owners' Equity

Basic Earnings per Share (Basic EPS)

Basic Earnings per Share is the Net Income of a firm over a period of time (quarter or year) divided by the weighted average number of shares of Common Stock outstanding over the same period.

.... **C** ....

Capital Expenditures

Capital Expenditures generally refer to purchases of long-lived or fixed assets, such as property, buildings, and equipment. Sometimes, Capital Expenditures are referred to as "capex." In the Statement of Cash Flows, Capital Expenditures will be shown as Cash for Investing Activities and will sometimes be called Property Acquired or a similar designation.

Capital Lease

A Capital Lease is a lease that requires the lessee to recognize the leased asset and the related lease liability on its Balance Sheet. Sometimes a Capital Lease is referred to as a "financing lease."

Capitalize

Capitalize is the process of increasing an asset account for a current or future expenditure. Items that meet the definition of an asset are generally Capitalized. An asset is an item that represents a probable future benefit to a firm. For example, inventory is Capitalized as an asset. The benefits of inventory are future sales. Inventory is subsequently "Expensed" when the benefits are received, that is, when the inventory is sold. Similarly, buildings are first Capitalized, and then they are expensed over future periods when the building is used. The Expense associated with using a building is Depreciation Expense.

Cash Cycle (or Days other Financing Required)

Cash Cycle = Operating Cycle – Days Payable Outstanding

Cash Flows from Financing Activities (CFF)

Cash Flows from Financing Activities are cash receipts and disbursement primarily from and to suppliers of capital, both debt capital and equity capital. CFF includes cash from stock issues, from bank borrowings, and from bond issues, and it includes cash payments to banks and bondholders for principal amounts borrowed and to shareholders for repurchases of stock and for dividend payments.

Cash Flows from Investing Activities (CFI)

Cash Flows from Investing Activities are cash receipts from sales of certain investments and various long lived assets (such as buildings and equipment and intangibles), as well as cash disbursements for purchases of such assets. Cash that is spent specifically to acquire property is generally referred to as "Capital Expenditures" or just "capex."

Cash Flows from Operations (CFO)

Cash Flows from Operations (also called Operating Cash Flows or Cash from Operating Activities) are primarily cash receipts and disbursements to and from other firms, entities, and individuals that are a part of the firm's central operations. These cash flows would include cash to suppliers of inventory, to employees, to the government for taxes, from sales to customers, etc.

Cash Interest Coverage

Cash Interest Coverage is calculated as: (Cash Flows from Operations + Cash Payments for Interest and Income Taxes) / Cash Payments for Interest.

Clean COGS

Clean COGS is an expression used by analysts that refers to Cost of Goods Sold without any depreciation. In a manufacturing environment, depreciation on factory equipment is capitalized as part of Work in Process Inventory. After Work in Process Inventory is completed and when the Finished Goods are sold, the Cost of Goods Sold will include the depreciation that was previously capitalized. Analysts remove the depreciation to obtain Clean COGS, which facilitates financial modeling.

Closing Entry

The Closing Entry is the Journal Entry that closes all temporary accounts. The temporary accounts (Revenues, Gains, Expenses and Losses) are closed in order to reset their respective balances to zero. After closing, the Temporary Accounts can begin accumulating the Revenues, Gains, Expenses and Losses for the next reporting period. Retained Earnings is part of the Closing Entry. When the Closing Entry is made, the amounts in the Temporary Accounts are transferred to Retained Earnings.

Common Size Ratios

Common Size ratios are ratios that convert raw, absolute data on the Income Statement and on the Balance Sheet to relative measures by dividing each data item on the Income Statement by total Sales and each item on the Balance Sheet by total Assets. The relative measure allows firms of different absolute sizes to be compared on a relative basis. For example, one firm may have $10 in Inventory and a second firm may have $100 in Inventory. On an absolute basis the second firm has more Inventory. If the first firm has total Assets of $30 and the second firm has total Assets of $1,000, then the first firm has more Inventory on a relative, or common-size basis. "Common-sizing" (that is, dividing by a common measure in the denominator, either total Sales or total Assets) is also referred to as "scaling" or "normalizing."

Common Stock

Common Stock is the most widely used form of equity financing. The holders of (investors in) Common Stock typically are given the right to vote on matters of governance of the firm.

Compound Interest

Compound Interest is interest that is calculated on original Principal, adjusted for any subsequent Accretion or Amortization.

Consolidation

Consolidation is the process of combining two or more sets of Financial Statements into one. Investors who exercise control over other firms will consolidate the Financial Statements of these firms with their own and report Consolidated Financial Statements of the group of firms.

Construction in Progress (CIP)

Construction in Progress is the cost of a fixed asset (such as a building) that a firm is building. Construction in Progress will include cost of materials, labor, various indirect costs associated with the construction process, as well as financing charges, such as interest.

Contra-accounts

Contra-accounts are accounts that re-value other accounts. They are used so that investors can determine the original value in the main account and the re-valuation that has been recognized to date or over a period of time. Contra-accounts are on the Balance Sheet and Income Statement. Examples of Contra-accounts on the Balance Sheet (and in parentheses, the accounts that they revalue) are: Accumulated Depreciation (Property, Plant, and Equipment), Allowance for Doubtful Accounts (Accounts Receivable), and Treasury Stock (Stock). Examples of Contra-accounts on the Income Statement are: Sales Returns, Sales Discounts, and Sales Allowances (Sales).

Cost Method

The Cost Method is a method for valuing Investments. Investments that are measured under the Cost Method are recognized in the Balance Sheet at their initial (historical) cost when they were purchased. For Investments in certain debt investments, such as Investments in another firm's bonds, the cost method would require that the investments be recognized at their original cost less any amortization of Discount or Premium.

Cost of Goods Sold (COGS)

Cost of Goods Sold represents the cost of Inventory that a firm sells to customers. COGS is an expense. Therefore, when COGS is recognized, Owners' Equity is decreased. The offset to the decrease in Owners' Equity is a corresponding decrease in Inventory. The value of COGS is determined by an Inventory costing method, such as FIFO (first-in-first-out), LIFO (last-in-first-out), Specific Identification or the Average Method.

Cost Principle

The Cost Principle is the principle that requires firms to recognize the full cost of acquiring assets. These costs would include the invoice price of the asset and any other costs necessary to acquire the asset and bring it to its place of use (such as shipping, insurance, and installation). Once the asset is recognized on the firm's Balance Sheet at its full cost, the asset may continue to be recognized in future periods at this initial (historical) cost, or at its initial cost less any adjustments for depreciation. However, certain assets must be marked-to-market and would therefore no longer be recognized at their historical costs.

Cost Ratio

Cost Ratio = Cost of Goods Sold / Sales

Credit

Credit is the right side of a journal entry, as well as the right side of a T-Account. Credits reduce asset accounts, but increase liability and Owners' Equity accounts.

Credit Rating

A credit rating is a rating (grade) assigned to a firm's debt by a credit rating agency. The grades typically are letters that indicate the firm's creditworthiness (that is, the ability of the firm to meet its obligations under a debt agreement). A rating of "AAA" is the highest rating and indicates the highest degree of creditworthiness. Below a certain rating, debt would be considered non-investment grade, sometimes referred to as "junk" or "high yield." Credit ratings affect the interest rate that firms would have to pay on new debt. A firm with a low credit rating would typically pay a higher interest rate on new debt than a firm with a high rating.

Credit Risk

Credit risk is the risk that a firm will not receive all amounts that it is owed by a borrower or by a customer who has purchased an asset on credit.

Current Assets

Current Assets are assets such as cash and other assets that will convert to cash, or will be used or consumed during the current year or operating cycle, whichever is longer. Examples of Current Assets include cash, Accounts Receivable, prepaid expenses, short term investments, and Inventory.

Current Liabilities

Current Liabilities are liabilities that are paid from Current Assets. Thus, they are typically liquidated within one year. Current Liabilities include accounts payable (amounts owed to suppliers), accrued liabilities (such as wages payable, rent payable, utilities payable, etc.), deferred revenue (which is expected to be earned over the next year), dividends payable (dividends declared but not yet paid), short term debt, and current maturities of long term debt.

Current Ratio

Current Ratio = Current Assets / Current Liabilities

.... **D** ....

Days Payable Outstanding (DPO)

Days Payable Outstanding = 365 Days / Accounts Payable Turnover (where 365 is the number of days in the period)

Days Sales in Inventory (DSI)

Days Sales in Inventory (DSI) = 365 Days / Inventory Turnover (where 365 is the number of days in the period)

Days Sales Outstanding (DSO)

Days Sales Outstanding (DSO) = 365 Days / Accounts Receivable Turnover (where 365 is the number of days in the period)

Debit

Debit is the left side of a journal entry, as well as the left side of a T-Account. Debits increase asset accounts, but decrease liability and Owners' Equity accounts.

Deferred Tax Assets

Deferred Tax Assets are estimated future income tax deductions (on a firm's tax return) multiplied by the Statutory Tax Rate. Deferred Tax Assets result from a difference between the Income Statement under GAAP and the Tax Return under the applicable tax laws. If GAAP requires that a firm recognize an expense in the current period, but the tax laws do not permit a corresponding deduction until a future period, then the firm will have a Deferred Tax Asset. Deferred Tax Assets can also arise from timing differences over when items are taxed, and not just when deductions are allowed.

Deferred Tax Liabilities

Deferred Tax Liabilities are estimates of increased income taxes to be paid to the government. Expected income tax increases could result from a firm exhausting income tax deductions in earlier periods. For instance, if a firm is allowed accelerated deductions for depreciation under applicable tax laws, but expenses a lesser amount for depreciation under GAAP, the firm will have a Deferred Tax Liability. The future higher taxes are due to the fact that the firm took the deduction in the current year, meaning future years will have no, or less, deduction available. Deferred Tax Liabilities can also arise from timing differences over when items are taxed, and not just when deductions are allowed.

Depreciate

Depreciate is the process of assigning a portion of the cost of fixed assets, such as buildings and equipment, to an Expense, called Depreciation Expense. When Depreciation Expense is recognized, Owners' Equity is reduced and the corresponding depreciable asset is also reduced. Usually the fixed asset account is reduced indirectly through the Contra-account called Accumulated Depreciation.

Diluted Earnings per Share (Diluted EPS)

Diluted Earnings per Share is "adjusted" Net Income of a firm over a period of time (quarter or year) divided by "adjusted" weighted average number of shares of Common Stock outstanding over the same period. The adjustments for Diluted EPS are for additional shares of Common Stock that could be issued under certain conditions. For instance, certain types of debt ("convertible bonds"), stock ("convertible preferred stock"), and stock options could become Common Stock if certain conditions are met. If convertible bondholders, convertible preferred stockholders, and owners of stock options were to become Common Stockholders, the number of shares of stock would increase, thereby diluting Basic EPS. Certain refinements are also made to the numerator for some of these convertible instruments.

Direct Materials (DM)

Direct Materials are Inventory items that a manufacturer uses in production of other Inventory. These are the raw (unfinished or unprocessed) materials that subsequent production processes convert to Finished Goods. Along with Work in Process and Finished Goods, Direct Materials inventory is one of three components of Inventory for a manufacturer.

Direct Method

Direct Method refers to a method for deriving Cash Flows from Operations. The Direct Method requires an analysis of all accounts related to a firm's operating activities in order to identify the changes attributable to cash flows. For example, Accounts Receivable is related to a firm's operating activities. The two primary effects on Accounts Receivable are credit sales (which increase Accounts Receivable) and cash collections from customers (which decrease Accounts Receivable). Cash collections from customers is one of the major components of Cash Flows from Operations. The procedure is repeated for all accounts related to a firm's operating activities, which include, for example, Inventory, prepaid expenses, accounts payable, taxes payable, and accrued operating expenses. The Direct Method is rarely used in practice. The other method for deriving Cash Flows from Operations is the Indirect Method.

Discount

"At a Discount" refers to bonds that are issued below Par Value. Bonds are issued at a Discount when the stated rate of interest (also called the coupon rate) is less than the market rate, that is, the rate the market requires for its investment in the bond.

Dividend Payout Ratio

Dividend Payout Ratio = Total Dividends / Net Income, or, on a per share basis, as Dividends per Share / Earnings per Share

Dividend Yield

Dividend Yield = Dividends per Share / Price per Share of Stock

Double Declining Balance

The Double Declining Balance method is a method for depreciating an asset, such as a building. It is referred to as an Accelerated Method, because more Depreciation Expense is taken early in the asset's life and less is taken later. The formula for Double Declining Balance is as follows: Depreciation Expense = (Cost – Accumulated Depreciation) x 2 x 1/life, where life is the expected useful life of the asset to the firm.

E

Earnings Before Interest and Taxes (EBIT)

Earnings Before Interest and Taxes is a subtotal on the Income Statement. It is often referred to as Operating Income or Operating Earnings. EBIT shows the central, ongoing results of a firm for a period of time. EBIT is measured as Sales – Cost of Goods Sold – Selling, General, and Administrative Expense – Research and Development Expense – Depreciation and Amortization. Thus, EBIT is measured before financing related expenses (Interest Expense) and Income Tax Expense.

Earnings Before Interest, Taxes, Depreciation, and Amortization (EBITDA)

EBITDA = Sales – Cost of Goods Sold – Selling, General, and Administrative Expenses – Research and Development Expenses Alternatively, EBITDA can be calculated as EBIT + Depreciation and Amortization. EBITDA is sometimes used as a rough estimate of Cash Flows from Operations. However, EBITDA does not include interest and taxes. (Interest and taxes are considered operating cash flows in the U.S.) Further, EBITDA does not incorporate changes in working capital accounts that are necessary to calculate Cash from Operating Activities.

Earnings per Share (EPS)

Earnings per Share is the Net Income of a firm over a period of time (quarter or year) per common stockholder. It shows how much of a firm's Net Income is attributable to each common stockholder. There are two main variations of EPS: Basic EPS and Diluted EPS.

EBIT Margin

EBIT Margin = Earnings Before Interest and Taxes / Sales

Effective Interest Rate (Pretax)

When referring to the average interest rate on a firm's debt, the Effective Interest Rate is sometimes estimated as **Interest Expense / Total Interest Bearing Debt**. If Total Interest Bearing Debt changes significantly over a period, Average Total Interest Bearing Debt is used in the denominator. The Effective Interest Rate also refers to the "yield to maturity", the "real rate", or the "required rate" of interest on a bond.

Effective Tax Rate

Effective Tax Rate = Income Tax Expense / Pretax Income (Income Tax Expense is often referred to as "Provision for Income Taxes.") Although the Effective Tax Rate is calculated from amounts on the Income Statement, it depends in part on calculations on the firm's income tax return. The Effective Tax Rate usually results from a mixture of income tax rates that are applied to a firm's income tax return. For instance, some items may be taxed at regular statutory rates, but other items may not ever be taxed at all, in which case the tax rate for that particular item is zero. Thus, the Effective Tax Rate is an average tax rate.

Equity Method

Equity Method is a method for accounting for investments in equity securities. The Equity Method is used when an investor has significant influence over the investee. Significant influence is reached at an ownership level that is above "passive" and below "control." Generally the passive ownership level is assumed to be less than about 20% of ownership, and control is over 50%.

Expense

Expense (as a verb) is the process of decreasing Owners' Equity for the recognition of an Expense, such as Cost of Goods Sold, Selling, General, and Administrative Expense, Depreciation Expense, etc.

.... **F** ....

Face Value

Face Value is the bond's maturity value. Face Value is a Future Value, or the amount that the bond issuer will pay the bondholder at maturity.

Fair Value Accounting

Fair Value Accounting is an accounting system that recognizes unrealized gains and losses for certain assets and liabilities. The recognition of the unrealized gains and losses will adjust the carrying value of the assets and liabilities to their respective fair values. Therefore, the assets and liabilities that are subject to Fair Value Accounting are shown on the Balance Sheet at their fair values (market values), rather than historical cost. Fair value accounting is also called mark-to-market accounting. If an asset that is subject to Fair Value Accounting was purchased for $10, and then rises in value to $15, the firm will increase the value of the asset by $5, with an offsetting increase to Owners' Equity. The offset in Owners' Equity is either a gain that is recognized in the current Income Statement or is a deferred gain that is held in Accumulated Other Comprehensive Income until the asset is sold.

FIFO (First-in-First-Out)

FIFO is an acronym that stands for First-In-First-Out. FIFO is a method for assigning costs of Inventory purchased or manufactured to Inventory that is sold. The costs of the first Inventory items purchased or produced are assigned to Cost of Goods Sold. If the first item in inventory cost $10 and the second cost $14, then, for the sale of a single item, Cost of Goods Sold is $10.

Financial Accounting Standards Board (FASB)

The Financial Accounting Standards Board is the organization that writes official accounting standards that are used in the U.S. The standards that the FASB writes are called Statements of Financial Reporting Standards. In the U.S., the FASB's authority to write standards is sanctioned by the Securities and Exchange Commission.

Financial Leverage

Financial Leverage is the presence of fixed-rate debt in the capital structure. The effect of Financial Leverage is to magnify the effects on Net Income that occur from changes in Revenues and Variable Operating Expenses. For instance if EBIT is $10 and Interest Expense is 5, then Income before Tax would be $5 ($10 – 5). Assuming a 40% tax rate, then Tax Expense is $2 ($5 x 40%) and Net Income is $3 ($5 – 2). If Revenues and Variable Operating Expenses all increase by 50%, EBIT will increase by 50%, from $10 to 15, since all Revenues and Variable Operating Expenses vary by the same or similar percentage. Since Interest Expense is fixed at $5, Income before Tax would be $10 ($15 – 5). Assuming a 40% tax rate, then Tax Expense is $4 ($10 x 40%) and Net Income is $6 ($10 – 4). EBIT increased by 50% (from $10 to $15), but Net Income increased by 100% (from $3 to $6). The reason Net Income increased by more than EBIT, in percentage terms, is the effect of Financial Leverage.

Finished Goods (FG)

Finished Goods is the end product of the production process for a manufacturer. Finished Goods inventory follows Direct Materials and Work in Process in the flow of Inventory items for a manufacturer. Finished Goods are sold to customers.

Form 10-K

Form 10-K is the name of the annual filing that publicly traded firms are required to make in the U.S. with the Securities and Exchange Commission. It contains the Financial Statements, information about the firm's industry and risk factors, and several other items that the Securities and Exchange Commission mandates to try to ensure full and fair disclosure about the firm for investors.

Form 10-Q

Form 10-Q is the name of the quarterly filing that publicly traded firms are required to make with the Securities and Exchange Commission. Form 10-Q contains the quarterly Financial Statements and several other disclosures, but it is not as comprehensive as the annual filing (Form 10-K).

Form 8-K

Form 8-K is the name of the filing that publicly traded firms are required to make whenever there is a material, current event about which investors should be informed. Form 8-K is mandated by the Securities and Exchange Commission (SEC) so that investors are made aware of material events on a more timely basis than quarterly or yearly. Some major events are specified by the SEC, but others require the firm to exercise judgment about whether the events are relevant for investors and therefore require disclosure. Firms are also required to furnish their earnings announcements on Form 8-K.

Future Value

Future Value is the value in the future of an amount deposited or loaned today. Future Values include any accretion of interest or amortization of Principal. For example, the Future Value of $100 that is deposited at a bank today is $121 in two years, if the bank pays 10% interest per year. $121 includes the accretion $10 of interest in the first year and $11 in the second year. The Future Value of $1,050 that is borrowed today but paid off over 2 years with two equal payments of $605 is 0. $605 is the exact amount needed to pay interest of 10% and Principal over 2 years so that the loan's balance after two years (the future value) is zero.

·· G ··

GAAP

GAAP is an acronym that stands for Generally Accepted Accounting Principles, which are written and promulgated by standard setting bodies. In the U.S., the Financial Accounting Standards Board is the official standard setting body. The International Accounting Standards Board is another standard setting body. Publicly traded firms must adhere to GAAP and have their Financial Statements audited by an independent audit firm to determine whether the Financial Statements "present fairly" the financial condition and results of operation of the firm in accordance with GAAP. GAAP requires firms to exercise judgment in some cases, and GAAP also allows firms to choose among different accounting treatments and methods.

Gains

Gains are increases to Owners' Equity that result from peripheral (not central and ongoing) activities of a firm. There are two types of Gains: realized and unrealized. A realized Gain can occur, for example, when a firm actually sells an asset to another firm for an amount that is greater than the value of the asset on the Balance Sheet. For instance, if a firm has an asset with a book value of $100 that it sells for $110, the firm would have a realized Gain of $10. An unrealized Gain can occur when a firm recognizes an increase in value of an asset but it does not sell the asset. If a firm has an asset with a book value of $100 that increases in value by $10, the firm would have an unrealized Gain of $10. Unrealized Gains are also called "paper gains." Unrealized Gains are recognized under Fair Value Accounting for certain classes of assets and liabilities.

Goodwill

Goodwill is the amount of a purchase price of a firm that exceeds the purchased firm's fair value. An acquiring firm may be willing pay more than fair value for another firm in order to obtain special synergies that could arise from the two firms being combined. For instance, if the net fair value of a firm (fair value of identifiable assets less the fair value of liabilities) is $10, and another firm acquires 100% of it by paying $12, Goodwill is $2. Goodwill is carried in the Balance Sheet as an intangible asset at its originally assigned value, but it is tested annually for Impairment.

Gross Margin

*Gross Margin = (Sales – Cost of Goods Sold) / Sales
The Cost Ratio and Gross Margin add up to "1". If a firm has Sales of $100 and Cost of Goods Sold of $60, then Gross Margin (sometimes referred to as Gross Margin Ratio) is 40%, or: (100 – 60) / 100. The Cost Ratio, **Cost of Goods Sold / Sales**, in this instance is 60%, or: 60 / 100.*

Gross Profit

Gross Profit is defined as Sales less Cost of Goods Sold. If a firm has Sales of $100 and Cost of Goods Sold of $60, the Gross Profit is $40. Gross Profit is the numerator of the Gross Margin Ratio.

.... I ....

Impairment Loss

Impairments are reductions in the values of assets from their recognized values in the Balance Sheet (also called book values or carrying values) to their new, lower fair values. The offset to the reduction in the asset is a reduction to Owners' Equity for the Impairment Loss. For instance, if the book value of an asset is $10, but the fair value is $4, the asset is impaired and written down by $6, with an offsetting Impairment Loss recognized in the Income Statement. When significant, Impairment Losses are typically shown in the Income Statement as a special "line item." However, sometimes Impairment Losses are included as operating expenses and included in Selling, General, and Administrative Expenses. In some accounting regimes, reversals of Impairment Losses are allowed.

Income Statement

The Income Statement is one of the three primary financial statements (besides the Balance Sheet and the Statement of Cash Flows). The Income Statement contains all of a firm's Revenues, Expenses, Gains and Losses. The sum of Revenues and Gains less Expenses and Losses is a firm's Net Income for a reporting period (such as a quarter or a year). Net Income is transferred to Retained Earnings at the end of every reporting period. The transfer to Retained Earnings is made via the Closing Entry, which is the Journal Entry that closes all Revenue, Gain, Expense, and Loss accounts, which are temporary accounts.

Indirect Method

The Indirect Method refers to a method for deriving Cash Flows from Operations(CFO). The Indirect Method removes from Net Income all non-cash components, such as non-cash Revenues (such as credit sales), and non-cash Expenses (such as depreciation and accrued expenses). The Indirect Method also removes all Gains and Losses, since these amounts, by definition, do not pertain to operating activities, nor do they correspond to the cash flow in the event that gives rise to the Gain or Loss. The algebraic formula for the Indirect Method is as follows: ***Cash Flows from Operations (CFO) = Net Income + Depreciation and Amortization Expense + Losses – Gains – Changes in CFO-Related Assets + Changes in CFO-Related Liabilities***, where CFO-Related Assets include, for example, Accounts Receivable, Prepaid Expenses, and Inventory, and CFO-Related Liabilities include, for example, accounts payable, taxes payable, and accrued operating expenses. If a firm has Net Income of $100, Depreciation Expense of $5, a gain of $7, a loss of $2, Increases in Accounts Receivable of $8, Decreases in Inventory or $6, and Increases in Accounts Payable of $9, then CFO is calculated as follows: ***CFO =100+5-7+2-8+6+9=107***. Notably, increases (decreases) in CFO-related Assets are subtracted (added); conversely, increases (decreases) in CFO-related Liabilities are added (subtracted). The other method for deriving Cash Flows from Operations is the Direct Method. The Indirect Method is the more commonly used method.

Initial Public Offering (IPO)
Initial Public Offering is the first sale of stock to public investors.

Interest Coverage
Interest Coverage = EBIT / Interest Expense

International Accounting Standards Board (IASB)
The International Accounting Standards Board is the organization that writes official accounting standards that are used in most of the world. The standards that the IASB writes are called International Financial Reporting Standards (IFRS).

Inventory
Inventory consists of items purchased or manufactured for re-sale to customers. Inventory for a manufacturer consists of Direct Materials, Work in Process, and Finished Goods. Inventory for a retailer is often called Merchandise Inventory.

Inventory Turnover
Inventory Turnover = Cost of Goods Sold / Inventory. When Inventory changes significantly over a period, average Inventory is used in the denominator.

Investments
Investments are generally either debt instruments (such as bonds) or shares of stock that one firm purchases of another. The Investments are initially recognized at cost when they are purchased. The subsequent accounting treatment depends on the type of Investment and how the Investments are classified. Depending on the classification, some Investments remain at historical cost, whereas others may be marked-to-market and therefore carried at fair value.

Investors
Investors are individuals or organizations that buy the stock of a firm. The stock represents ownership of the firm. Thus, investors become the firm's owners. (In some contexts, "Investors" is a term that is applied much more broadly and includes not only the owners of stock, but also the owners of a firm's debt. In this broader context therefore, Investors would include any individual or organization that supplies any type of outside capital or financing to a firm.)

J

Journal Entries
Journal entries are the means by which accounting events are initially captured in the financial system. Journal Entries consist of at least two parts, and they must always balance. For instance, an increase in an asset must be offset by a decrease in another asset, or by an increase in a liability or an owners' equity account, or some combination of the above.

L

Lease
A Lease is an arrangement where one party (the lessee) rents an asset from another (the lessor). The lessor is the owner of the asset. For accounting purposes, there are two types of Leases: Capital and Operating. Capital Leases are capitalized by the lessee, meaning that the lessee recognizes the leased asset and the lease liability in its Balance Sheet at the inception of the Lease. Operating Leases are called "off-

balance-sheet" Leases because the lessee does not recognize the leased asset and lease liability, rather only periodic lease (rent) expense.

Ledger

The Ledger is the name of the registry where the account balances are calculated and stored. The amounts from the Journal Entries are transferred ("posted") to the individual accounts stored in the Ledger. The posted amounts are then added to existing data from earlier Journal Entries to determine the account balances.

Lenders

Lenders are individuals or organizations that loan money to borrowers. The amount loaned is called the Principal. Borrowers repay lenders the Principal and Interest. Lenders include banks, other firms, and bondholders.

Leverage

Leverage is a general term that describes the amount of debt that a firm has in its capital structure. Various ratios measure Leverage, such as Debt-to-Capital, which is **Total Interest Bearing Debt / (Total Interest Bearing Debt + Owners' Equity)**. If used in the "DuPont Method" (which measures Return on Equity in three factors), **Leverage = Total Assets / Owners' Equity**. Leverage ratios show how much debt capital, rather than equity capital, is used in the capital structure of the firm. Leverage has certain benefits that a firm finds advantageous over equity, but "too much" leverage can limit a firm's financial flexibility. Thus, firms attempt to find the "optimal" amount of Leverage for their particular situation.

LIFO (Last-in-First-Out)

LIFO is an acronym that stands for Last-In-First-Out. LIFO is a method for assigning costs of inventory purchased or manufactured to Inventory that is sold. The costs of the last Inventory items purchased or produced are assigned to Cost of Goods Sold. If the first item in inventory cost $10 and the second cost $14, then, for the sale of a single item, Cost of Goods Sold is $14.

Liquidity

Liquidity refers to a firm's cash position and the ability to convert other assets to cash quickly if needed. For example, short-term investments can usually be converted to cash (sold) quickly. In the U.S., assets are reported on the Balance Sheet in order of liquidity, with the most liquid assets shown first (cash) and the least liquid assets shown last (intangible assets).

Losses

Losses are decreases to Owners' Equity that result from peripheral (not central and ongoing) activities of a firm. There are two types of Losses: realized and unrealized. A realized Loss can occur, for example, when a firm sells an asset to another firm for an amount that is less than the value of the asset on the Balance Sheet. For instance, if a firm has an asset with a book value of $100 that it sells for $90, the firm would have a realized Loss of $10. An unrealized Loss can occur when a firm recognizes a decrease in value of an asset, but it does not sell the asset. If a firm has an asset with a book value of $100 that decreases in value by $10, the firm would have an unrealized Loss of $10. Unrealized Losses are also called "paper losses." Unrealized Losses are recognized under Fair Value Accounting for certain classes of assets and liabilities.

Lower of Cost or Market

Lower of Cost or Market is a test that is applied to Inventory at every reporting date. The test varies somewhat in different accounting regimes. The basic idea is that if Inventory is on the Balance Sheet at a cost that is higher than its "market value," then Inventory is written down to market. If Inventory must be reduced to a market value, the offset to the reduction in Inventory is a corresponding reduction in Owners' Equity, either as a Loss or as another amount included in Cost of Goods Sold. Lower of Cost or Market is an impairment test for Inventory.

M

Management Discussion and Analysis (MD&A)

Management Discussion & Analysis (MD&A) is a section of the 10-K (in the U.S.) that is mandated by the Securities and Exchange Commission. Firms must describe in the MD&A the reasons for major changes in the Financial Statements. For instance, management must discuss the reasons for changes in revenues and various expense categories. Also, firms must discuss plans for Capital Expenditures over the next twelve months, liquidity needs over the next twelve months, and any known trends and uncertainties, both favorable and unfavorable, that may affect future operations, liquidity, and financial position. The MD&A augments the Financial Statements by providing lenders, investors, and other interested parties management's insights about both the firm's past and expectations for the future.

Market Capitalization

Market Capitalization is usually calculated as the **Number of Shares of Common Stock Outstanding x Price per Share**. Market Capitalization is often referred to as "market cap."

Mark-to-Market Accounting

See **Fair Value Accounting**.

Matching Principle

The Matching Principle is one of the two main principles (besides the Revenue Principle) that underlies Accrual Accounting. The Matching Principle dictates when the firm recognizes Expenses. Expenses are recognized when they are incurred, meaning that they are recognized when the related Revenues are recognized. The name "matching" refers to the fact that expenses are necessary to generate Revenue and are therefore matched with Revenue in the same period.

Maturity

Maturity is the date when the Principal amount of debt is due to the lender.

.... **N** ....

Net Income

Net Income is the sum of all Revenues and Gains less all Expenses and Losses.

Net Operating Profit After Tax (NOPAT)

Net Operating Profit After Tax (NOPAT) = EBIT x (1-Effective Tax Rate). NOPAT is used in the calculation of Return on Invested Capital (ROIC).

Net Realizable Value

Net Realizable Value is the difference between Accounts Receivable and the Allowance for Doubtful

Accounts. It is also called "Net Receivable." Net Realizable Value is the amount of the Accounts Receivable that a firm expects to "realize" as payment (cash) from customers or borrowers.

New York Stock Exchange (NYSE)

The New York Stock Exchange is where stock and other Investments are traded (bought and sold) among buyers and sellers.

Non-recurring Items

Non-recurring Items are typically items that are unusual or infrequent events. Non-recurring Items are typically recognized in the Income Statement, "below The Line."

Note Disclosures

Note Disclosures are required disclosures that firms make in the notes to the Financial Statements. Contrasted with Note Disclosures are statement disclosures, which are required disclosures that firms make in the Financial Statements. The standard setters (such as the Financial Accounting Standards Board and the International Accounting Standards Board) typically have recognition thresholds that must be met for a required disclosure to become a statement disclosure. Note Disclosures do not meet these thresholds, and they typically augment statement disclosures by providing additional information about a firm's application of Generally Accepted Accounting Principles.

Note Receivable

A Note Receivable is generally a longer term receivable from a customer or borrower. Notes Receivable typically charge interest, whereas shorter-term receivables, such as Accounts Receivable, typically do not.

.... **O** ....

Operating Cycle

Operating Cycle = Days Sales Outstanding + Days Sales in Inventory

Operating Lease

An Operating Lease is a lease that does not require Balance Sheet recognition by the lessee. Operating Leases are often called "off balance sheet financing." The lessee has the right to use the leased asset, but it does not show the asset or the liability on the Balance Sheet.

Ordinary Annuity

An Ordinary Annuity is a series of cash payments made at the end of each period.

.... **P** ....

Par Value

Par Value is another name for face value of a bond or share of stock. If referring to a bond, Par Value is the amount that the bond issuer must pay the bond holder at maturity.

Preferred Stock

Preferred Stock is stock that confers upon the stockholder certain preferences not available to the holders of Common Stock. These preferences may include the option to convert from Preferred Stock to Common Stock, the ability to receive dividends prior to the holders of Common Stock, and the preference of receiving claims in bankruptcy prior to holders of Common Stock.

Premium

Premium refers to bonds that are issued above Par Value. Bonds are issued at a Premium when the Stated Rate of interest (also called the coupon rate) is greater than the rate that the market requires for its investment in the bond.

Present Value

Present Value is the value of cash today. For instance, Present Value is the amount of a deposit that would be required today to have a certain desired amount in the future. If a firm wants to have $121 in 2 years and can earn 10% per year on a deposit at a bank, the firm would need to deposit $100 today. The Present Value of $100 will grow by $10 for the first year and by $11 over the second year (11 = 10% x 110), resulting in $121 in 2 years. Present Value is also the amount that a lender is willing to loan to a firm today in return for the promise of future payments that include interest, as well as amount of the Principal.

Pro Forma Statements

Pro Forma statement are forecasted Financial Statements. Pro Forma means "for the sake of form." Pro Forma Statements are created by financial analysts to estimate what a firm will look like in the future.

Profit Margin

Profit Margin = Net Income / Sales

Proxy

The Proxy is the firm's announcement of its annual meeting for shareholders. The Proxy informs investors about the time and location of the meeting, as well as items on which investors are asked to vote. In the U.S., the Proxy is officially listed on the Securities and Exchange Commission's website as "Def 14A", where "Def" refers to "Definitive Proxy" under the relevant section of the securities code. The Proxy also contains extensive disclosures about executive compensation.

Purchases

"Purchases" is calculated as **Ending Inventory + Cost of Goods Sold – Beginning Inventory**. The amount for Purchases is used in Accounts Payable Turnover.

.... **Q** ....

Quick Ratio

Quick Ratio = Liquid Current Assets / Current Liabilities. Liquid Current Assets include cash, marketable securities, and short term receivables.

.... **R** ....

R&D Ratio

The R&D Ratio = Research and Development Expense / Sales

Restructurings

Restructurings are reductions in work force, cancelation of leases, or other types of changes in contracts or other agreements that will likely require payments to other parties, such as severance pay for workers or cancelation fees to lessors. Restructurings require that the firm recognize an expense or loss before payment. Thus, the offset to the reduction in Owners' Equity from recognition of the restructuring expense or loss is an increase in a liability.

Retained Earnings

Retained Earnings is the account on a firm's Balance Sheet in owners' equity that contains all of the firm's Net Income since the firm's inception, less the cumulative amount of dividends that the firm has declared.

Return on Assets (ROA)

*Return on Assets is defined as Net Income / Total Assets. Alternatively, it is the first two terms of the DuPont Method, or Net Income / Sales * Sales / Total Assets. See Return on Equity (ROE).*

Return on Equity (ROE)

Return on Equity = Net Income / Owners' Equity. Alternatively, using the DuPont Method, it is Net Income / Sales x Sales / Total Assets x Total Assets / Owners' Equity. The names of the three factors in the DuPont Method are, respectively, Profit Margin, Asset Turnover, and Leverage.

Return on Invested Capital (ROIC)

Return on Invested Capital (ROIC) is calculated as NOPAT / Invested Capital. Invested Capital is usually measured as the market values of total interest bearing debt and stock.

Revenue Principle

The Revenue Principle is one of the two main principles (besides the Matching Principle) that underlies accrual accounting. The Revenue Principle dictates when a firm is allowed to recognize Revenues. Although Revenue recognition can be complex in certain instances, the main notion is that firms are allowed to book Revenue when the earnings process is essentially complete and the customer has paid or is likely to pay the firm.

Revenues

Revenues are primarily inflows of assets from the firm's central, ongoing activities. Revenues are also called sales. When recognized, Revenues increase owners' equity. The offset to the recognition of Revenues is typically either cash or Accounts Receivable. If cash is the offset, then the firm has made a cash sale. If Accounts Receivable is the offset, then the firm had made a credit sale.

Revenues are recognized in accordance with the Revenue Recognition Principle.

·········· **S** ··········

Sales Allowance

Sales Allowance is a contra-account to sales. The Sales Allowance account is a temporary account whose balance is the value of reductions in selling price for a previously recorded sale. Sales Allowances are sometimes granted to customers as an incentive so that a customer will not return merchandise previously purchased. Similar to Sales Discounts and Sales Returns, Sales Allowances are typically disclosed as a Note Disclosure and sales are shown on the Income Statement as "Net Sales."

Sales Discount

Sales Discount is a contra-account to sales. The Sales Discount account is a temporary account whose balance is the value of discounts that the firm has granted to its customers to encourage early payment. Similar to Sales Returns and Sales Allowances, Sales Discounts are typically disclosed as a Note Disclosure and sales are shown on the Income Statement as "Net Sales."

Sales Return

Sales Returns is a contra-account to sales. The Sales Return account is a temporary account whose balance is the value of previously recorded sales that a customer has returned. Similar to Sales Discounts and Sales Allowances, Sales Returns are typically disclosed as a Note Disclosure and sales are shown on the Income Statement as "Net Sales."

Seasoned Equity Offerings (SEO)

Seasoned Equity Offerings are subsequent sales of stock in a firm. SEOs follow Initial Public Offerings.

Securities and Exchange Commission (SEC)

The U.S. Securities and Exchange Commission is the governmental agency that is primarily responsible for enforcing federal securities laws. The SEC's charge is to ensure that investors and potential investors have timely access to relevant financial information about an Investment before making a decision to buy or sell the Investment.

SG&A Ratio

SG&A Ratio = Selling, General, and Administrative Expense / Sales

Specific Identification Method

Specific Identification Method is a method for identifying the cost of items of Inventory that are sold. It is typically used only in firms who sell special or unique items. The cost of the actual item that is sold becomes the Cost of Goods Sold. The other major methods to identify the cost of items sold are LIFO, FIFO, and Average. For instance, if a firm has 1 item of Inventory that costs $18, a second that costs $21, and a third that costs $30, and then sells the second item, the Cost of Goods Sold is $21, using Specific Identification.

Stated Rate

The Stated Rate of interest is the interest rate that is stated as part of the bond contract. The Stated Rate (also called the coupon rate or the nominal rate) is compared to the market rate of interest (also called the yield to maturity, the real rate, the effective rate, or the required rate) to determine if the bond sells at a Discount, at a Premium, or at Par Value. The Stated Rate is multiplied by the Par Value of the bond to compute the amount of the coupon payment. If a bond has a $1,000 Par Value and a Stated Rate of interest of 5%, then the bond will pay $50 per year to the bondholder (50=5% x 1,000).

Statement of Cash Flows

The Statement of Cash Flows (SCF) is one of the three main Financial Statements (besides the Balance Sheet and the Income Statement). The SCF shows three categories of cash flows: Cash from Operating Activities, Cash from Investing Activities, and Cash from Financing Activities. The sum of these three categories equals the change in the cash account from one Balance Sheet to the subsequent Balance Sheet.

Statutory Tax Rate

The Statutory Tax Rate is the official, enacted tax rate of a tax jurisdiction, such as a federal government.

Strike Price

The Strike Price is the price that an owner of a stock option would be required to pay a firm for one share of its stock. If the strike price is lower than the firm's current stock price, the option is considered to be "in-the-money" and the option holder would likely exercise the option, because he or she can buy the stock at a discount. If the strike price is the same as or greater than the stock's current price, the option is "at-the-money" or "out-of-the money," respectively. An "out-of-the-money" option is also called an "underwater" option. Another name for Strike Price is option price.

-------------------------------- T --------------------------------

T-Account

T-Account is the form of an account using conventional methods. The left side of the "T" is the Debit side and the right side is the Credit side. The alternative to a T-Account is an equation. Both a T-Account and an equation show the beginning balances, increases and decreases in the account, and the ending balances.

Temporary Accounts

Temporary Accounts are all the Revenue, Gain, Expense, and Loss accounts. They are called temporary because their account balances are temporary. Temporary accounts are closed at the end of every reporting period via the Closing Entry. Temporary accounts are closed to re-set their balances to zero so that they can begin accumulating Revenues, Gains, Expenses and Losses for the next reporting period.

Temporary Difference

A Temporary Difference is a difference in the current period between the components of GAAP Financial Statements and the corresponding components of a firm's income tax returns. For instance, Revenues booked in the current period under GAAP may be taxed in periods other than the current period. Similarly, Expenses booked in the current period under GAAP may be deductible on the tax return in periods other than the current period. Temporary differences between GAAP statements and tax returns give rise to Deferred Tax Assets and Deferred Tax Liabilities.

The Line

The Line is an expression used by analysts that refers to Operating Income, or Earnings Before Interest and Taxes (EBIT). The significance of The Line is that all items above it, such as Sales, Cost of Goods Sold, SG&A Expense, and Depreciation Expense, are part of central, ongoing operations of the firm and therefore more likely to persist.

Total Debt to Capital

Total Debt to Capital = Total Interest Bearing Debt / (Total Interest Bearing Debt + Owners' Equity). Interest bearing debt includes short term and long term bank loans, current maturities of long term debt, and bonds.

Total Return to Shareholders (TRS)

Total Return to Shareholders = (Change in Stock Price per Share + Dividends paid per Share) / Stock Price at the Beginning of the Period

Trading Securities

Trading Securities are investments in securities that a firm purchases for the short term. Trading Securities are reported in the Balance Sheet as Current Assets and are carried at Fair Value. When their values change, the firm recognizes unrealized Gains and Losses as a component of the Income Statement.

Tranche

A Tranche is a slice of debt that has certain characteristics that distinguish it from other slices of debt. Examples of distinctive characteristics include length of maturity, interest rates, and credit ratings.

Treasury Stock

Treasury Stock is a contra-account in Owners' Equity. Treasury Stock is the value of stock that a firm has repurchased from its own shareholders. Generally, the value of Treasury Stock is the amount that the firm had to pay its shareholders to repurchase the shares (that is, the cost of the shares purchased).

.... V ....

Variable Operating Expenses

Variable Operating Expenses are expenses that vary directly with Revenues. If Revenues increase (decrease), Variable Operating Expenses also generally increase (decrease), although perhaps not by the exact same percentage.

.... W ....

Work in Process (WIP)

Work in Process is the inventory that is in the process of being converted to Finished Goods. Work in Process Inventory includes raw materials that have been transferred from Direct Materials Inventory, as well as Direct Labor, and Indirect Manufacturing costs, which is also called Overhead. Along with Direct Materials and Finished Goods, Work in Process is one of three components of Inventory for a manufacturer.

.... Y ....

Yield

The Yield generally refers to the interest rate implied by the price of a bond and the bond's cash flows. It shows the rate of return that a bondholder would actually earn, given how much the bondholder had to pay for the bond and given the future cash receipts from the bond, namely the coupon interest payments and the Par Value. The Yield is more specifically referred to as the "yield-to-maturity" and commonly referred to as the "Effective Rate of Interest." If a bond cost a bondholder $980 and pays $50 of interest for two years and then $1,000 Par Value at the end of two years, the Yield on the bond is 6.1%. The Yield is calculated by using the "rate" function in Excel. In this case, the parameters would be as follows: *=rate(nper, pmt, pv, fv); =rate(2,50,-980,1000).*